DIGITAL FRONTIER
Job & Opportunity Finder

Tomorrow's Opportunities Today

Don Altman

MOON LAKE MEDIA
LOS ANGELES, CA

... this book may be reproduced
... by any means, electronic or
...opying, recording, or by any
...rieval system–except by a
...f passages in a review to be
...newspaper–without express
...: publisher. For information
...Box 251466, Los Angeles, CA
90025.

First Printing 1996

While the author and publisher have done everything possible to find new
and interesting jobs, opportunities, and careers, we assume no responsibility
or liability for inaccuracies, errors, omissions, inconsistencies, or products
and services rendered in the creation of any and all of the ideas in this book.
Any slights of people, jobs, or organizations are fully unintentional. When
deciding on how to choose a job, decide upon opportunities, or conduct all
aspects of a career search, readers must use their own best judgment and
should consult with other reference sources and consultants if necessary.

Library of Congress Cataloging-in-Publication Data

Altman, Don, 1950-
    Digital frontier job & opportunity finder /
 Don Altman.
        p.   cm.
    Includes index.
        ISBN 0-9639161-1-4 (pbk. : alk. recycled paper)
        1. Information technology--Vocational guidance.
 I. Title.
 T58.5.A57   1996
 004'.023--dc20   95-40433
                                                                  CIP

Printed in the United States of America

ACKNOWLEDGMENTS:

Thanks to all friends and family for their feedback and help in my efforts to complete this book. In particular: Michael Arlen of Arlen Advertising, Ridgie Barton, Randy Fitzgerald, Dennis Miller, John Morley, James Oliver, Steven Ray, Michele Rifkin, Susan White, Old Eyes and Weese; Sanda Sein, the love of my life; with special thanks to my father Norman, mother Barabara, sister Cindy, Paul, and Debbie.

Special gratitude goes to my brother Jimmy for his fine research assistance on this book, and in general for always giving freely of his time, energy, and laughter.

PREFACE:

This book about prospecting for opportunities and jobs in the digital frontier does more than just answer the question "what are the latest, newest jobs for which to train and prepare?" It explores where we are going as a country, a society, and a people. Finding secure and long lasting gainful employment is no longer a given. Corporations down size, people move, and jobs shift like the proverbial wind. Just as our early ancestors once migrated with the seasons for survival, today we are a work force on-the-move, shifting from industry to industry and following new opportunities as old job markets dry up and disappear.

Change, ironically, has become the immutable touchstone guiding our futures. Knowing information age trends and how to locate and identify areas of need have become new and important skills. This book attempts to make that task easier by consolidating those new and available opportunities in the digital realm. Some are jobs that will one day be commonplace; some may peak quickly and become obsolete; still others may metamorphose into different jobs altogether. That is the beauty of a dynamic economy.

For those seeking results, take heart in knowing that the jobs will be there. This book attests to that. Getting the right training, along with networking and fostering the right attitude are the keys to maximizing the information in this book.

FOREWORD:

I thought Don was attempting an insurmountable task when he initially told me about his idea for this book. How can you make sense out of such a broad area that changes daily? This book is how. It avoids the trap of bogging down in the details that are changing daily to focus on the trends that are driving the new and expanding job market. But this isn't a bunch of ivory-tower predictions either. Each area of job opportunity is supported with at least one example of people making it work for themselves right now and creating jobs for others in the process.

A concern that others may have is that the term "digital" is too arbitrary or that it necessarily limits the scope of this book to computer-related jobs. The reality, as established by virtually every pundit and futurist currently in print, is that the world is well into the beginning of a socio-economic revolution every bit as far-reaching as the industrial revolution.

To a large extent the digital revolution is already into the next wave. The first wave was dominated by computer experts. Their expertise was critical to making the technology small enough to fit on a desktop and powerful enough to be of practical use. Now that these digital tools exist, the next wave demands people who can apply them to virtually every aspect of business and personal life.

Soon, utility meters may be read from a remote location, and that information automatically fed into a computer program that sends out your monthly bill– untouched, unseen, un-thought-about by any human. Whether or not this is good news for your career depends on whether you're a meter reader or part of a company that provides the digitally-based utility billing system. And that digitally-based utility billing system company needs the same range of employees as any other business, from sales people to installers to customer service reps and custodial workers– not just computer programmers, although they're needed too.

This book then is a guide to job opportunities in this next wave. It provides a consistent overview of the entire digital frontier, available nowhere else. Its tone of adventurous optimism sets an example of the attitude that has already helped the initial pioneers find success. Its organization and high-level overview helps you step back and see how all the pieces fit together and where your expertise may fit in.

Even if you spend all day at a computer, developing software products and writing about emerging digital technologies as I do, you'll gain new insights and enthusiasm from reading this book.

Though impressively accurate in its grasp of how digital technology changes all aspects of our world, it is not a book about technology. Instead it's a book about the full range of jobs and opportunities now emerging in a world that is already changing from anything that even a recent education could have prepared us for.

—John Morley
Co-Author, The Emerging Digital Future

TABLE OF CONTENTS:

SECTION I
Digital Frontier Overview

SECTION II
Networking Resource Guide

Introduction

WHO CAN USE THIS BOOK?

This book is intended for anyone looking to jump-start their future. That includes youthful newcomers entering the job market, seasoned workforce veterans, and anyone else searching for that new and exciting job or opportunity.

Guidance counselors will also find the contents a guide to emerging industries and trends. Jobs that were not in existence five or ten years ago are proliferating. New industries spring up to dot the working world's landscape in a matter of months. While the large corporations contribute their share of emerging jobs, many are being generated from small businesses and entrepreneurs.

Newly founded small businesses in emerging markets sometimes grow faster than established businesses. Start-ups also provide the opportunity to be part of the cutting edge, establish the ground rules, and be at the top of the food chain in a particular industry. All are excellent reasons to concentrate one's efforts in emerging job markets.

This book is organized in two sections. Section I paints a broad picture of the digital frontier and those major industries that comprise it. Each chapter covers jobs and opportunities within a specific industry. These include software and information services, hardware, on-line and communications services, creative services, advertising and marketing, and virtual reality.

Section II consists of a Networking Resource Guide– a practical tool filled with career and opportunity-specific information.

Sections I and II are designed to work together, and information is linked in a very straightforward way: Each chapter has its own dedicated resource. For example, if you're interested in Chapter 7 (virtual reality), just go to Resource 7 to locate associations, trade shows, conferences, publications, and training that's specific to the virtual reality industry.

At one time or another, you may have imagined being involved in work that goes beyond the ordinary in its ability to change the world. Hopefully, that work also provides you with a sense of security and respect. At least that's the dream. It is my hope that you find a little bit of that dream within these pages.

SECTION I

DIGITAL FRONTIER OVERVIEW

CHAPTER 1

DAWN OF A DIGITAL AGE

"You're as young as the last time you changed your mind." *Timothy Leary*

Stake Your Claim to the Future

So you always wanted to be a pioneer, prospector, or astronaut. You watched *Indiana Jones*, *Star Trek*, and *Star Wars*, knowing it was *you* who was destined to whoosh down a river with Indy, command the bridge of the Enterprise, and triumphantly kiss Princess Leia. If so, don't fret. Your chance to live out a real-life adventure on the digital frontier has arrived. Just choose your adventure, whether a prospector staking out precious territory or a commander launching new ideas and campaigns. Here's your turn to boldly stake claim to the uncharted future where few have gone before.

If you're so itchy to start that you can't wait another second, or if you already have a basic idea of the digital frontier areas, you can be daring and skip ahead to the next chapter. Sure, it's dangerous, but you're a rugged explorer who's just landed on the digital frontier. Besides, you can always come back to this outpost if you have to pick up some extra tips on reading the trail signs.

Welcome to the Frontier

For those of you who have decided to hang out while you get your cyber legs and adjust to the altitude, welcome to the frontier. Stow your gear and settle down for an overview of what to expect, overall trends that are shaping the frontier, and emerging territories that you may decide to visit. (Tours leave on the nanosecond.) In the meantime, we'll do our best to keep you away from those unsavory characters at the Techno-Babble Bar and Grill until you build up a tolerance. Before long, you'll be ready to stroll on in and toss out an acronym or two. Or three.

If you are not yet aware of it, you will soon discover that something wonderful is happening. We live at the dawn of a digital age that is changing the basic ways we work, shop, interact, entertain, and educate. Like the rebirth of art, science, and literature spreading throughout Europe at the half-point of the millennium, our 21st century digital dawn also sows the seeds of cultural, social, and economic treasures.

It's no exaggeration that the emerging digital frontier heralds some very real, if not downright revolutionary, shifts in jobs and opportunities. It's the chance for you to stake claim to a tangible piece of the digital frontier. But to do so, you'll need to toss out preconceived ideas of the way things have always been done.

This is Not Your Father's Frontier

The digital frontier encompasses several new outposts, or territories. And like the wild west of 150 years ago, there are no well paved roads, maps, and Triple A road service to help you when things go awry. More often than not there's the gnawing feeling that you have just entered the land of OZ.

You thought you understood job titles? Think again, because some digital job titles and responsibilities don't exist until they are made up– on the spot. Yesterday's graphic artist is today's *multimedia designer*, and yesterday's high-powered executive is today's *Manager of Technical Evangelism and Developer Relations* or *Vice President of Cool* (honest-to-goodness job titles at Microsoft and America Online, respectively).

Out on the far reaches of the frontier, on-line services even employ "digital talent scouts" whose job it is to scour the digital sandlots of cyber space, looking for hot prospects possessing major league quality content and ideas.

The size and nature of corporations seems foreign, too, as more corporate offices downsize and employees telecommute from home. Local and wide area networks link corporate offices together, providing real-time services and products to the corporation and customers alike. Videoconferencing, once the exclusive domain of off-site executive conference rooms, is cropping up in average looking offices.

For those of you who are boomers and gen-Xrs, the digital frontier is a major departure from the less volatile and stable work experience of the nostalgic '50s and '60s. The frontier is an idea mill, spinning out vivid and hip digital slang the instant it ramps onto the information highway. If you breach the Internet's code for proper "netiquette" you will be "flamed" with E-mail as retribution. The digital frontier is a nurturing place where verbs and nouns are not only born, but in fact bear offspring.

A Multimedia Bonanza

Out on the frontier, get ready for your senses to be tickled with new and experimental forms of digital art and entertainment. Virtual art galleries, interactive music CDs, and interactive multimedia novels push the envelope of traditional forms. Educators routinely use multimedia CD-ROMs to teach and track a student's progress.

That a single CD-ROM is capable of containing an encyclopedia of information that can be sorted and searched in a matter of seconds is as basic and profound a paradigm shift as was Johann Gutenberg's 15th century printing press. And that's just the tip of the iceberg.

The ability to combine text, sound, images, and video in an interactive format on the desktop creates a host of new corporate uses, from computer based training, or CBT, to customized sales and marketing tools. Salespersons can pick and choose from a menu of items to build instant presentations specially designed for a particular customer.

Turned On and Tuned In

The phenomenal capability of networking makes it possible to connect people, via their computers, in a myriad of unique associations and arrangements. If you've experienced on-line services like Prodigy, CompuServe, and America Online, then you have already pioneered cyber space, helping create and populate virtual cities filled with a cornucopia of services and products. This is no less than the birth of a new medium, where on-line services stand poised to give the TV networks competition for viewership and advertising dollars.

If you are especially brave, you may have visited the Internet, initially a highly technical, somewhat arcane and academic-oriented network of computers. Since the Internet gained greater accessibility through a unifying and linking tool known as the World Wide Web, it is expanding more rapidly than ever imagined. There are good reasons for this.

The new on-line medium is ideal for helping you reach out to experts and make business contacts around the world in ways otherwise not economically feasible. From on-line job searching to marketing and advertising, there's a whole untapped medium primed for opportunity seeking digital prospectors.

Data, Data, and More Data

Beyond the digital frontier's kaleidoscopic thrills and delights, however, are pioneering technologies that make it all possible. These technical boundaries are propelled forward by engineers and technicians who pave the way for the rest of us.

With so much happening simultaneously on so many fronts, one thing is certain: The digital dawn is already here. It is fed by a tremendous rush of excitement, vision, energy, and vast financial resources devoted to it at all levels, including government and large corporations, venture capitalists and start up infopreneurs, and even Johnny the neighborhood kid who programs computer games in his garage. And of course, frontier rebel rousers like yourself.

A Digital Paradigm Shift

The lifeblood of any new age depends on new forms and paradigm shifts. A "frontier," however, implies the systematic structuring of an undeveloped region or field beyond known borders. It implies new settlements and hints of a newly drawn map with lots of space for pioneering settlers. That's where you come in.

As you read the map of territories and opportunities that this book draws, you will notice that these overlap and sometimes converge. The lines on this map are in flux, with mergers and alliances being commonplace.

Look at the business section of any local newspaper, and you'll witness the constant ebb and flow of digital business news. The speed with which these factors shift is dizzying. As the following statistics clearly acclaim, nothing matches the difficulty of predicting change on the digital frontier.

File these stats under the "Woefully obsolete by the time you read them" category

- 20-30 million consumer on-line users by 1997 or 1998
  Predicted June 1994, Folio Magazine

- 30 million Internet users in 1994, growing to 550 million in year 2000
  Dow Jones estimate

- 25% of US houses with home offices
  Predicted July 1995, Morph's Outpost

- 33.2 million CD-ROM drives installed in 1994, growing to 129.9 million drives in 1998
  Freeman Associates

- 180 million computers connected in the year 2000
  Internet Society

- 16.3 million installed multimedia computers in 1994, growing to 27.3 million in 1995
  SIMBA Information

- 17 million interactive CD-ROMs were shipped in 1993, growing to 54 million interactive CD-ROMs in 1994
  GISTICS Incorporated

- $10.7 billion total CD-ROM hardware and software revenues in 1994, growing to $18.1 billion in 1995
  InfoTech, Optical Publishing Industry

In case you haven't noticed, a favorite frontier hobby is bandying about the latest statistics and predictions. Everyone has a pet theory about what various numbers mean, and you'll want to develop your own as time goes by. Learn a few of them and you will be accepted into any outpost without proof of identification.

As for the statistics above? These may indicate that the massive influx and growth of on-line users have not weakened the CD-ROM market. That both these mediums can flourish simultaneously hints that they are being used for different purposes. Neither the Internet nor on-line consumer services are fully game, sound, video, and interactive ready. But that time is coming soon.

Keep in mind that these numbers pale in comparison with the number of TV and video watchers worldwide. But also remember that the digital frontier, while still growing, will not live or die on recreational uses, but by providing a full range of services and products. Some may eventually co-opt or merge with existing services like phone and TV.

Digital is Everywhere, Every Day in Every Way

If you have any doubt that the digital revolution is here full force, look around at a typical day's activities. That telephone you use at home is probably an analog device. Nonetheless, digital phone lines are cropping up all over. They allow high speed data transmission, can carry video and sound, and will revolutionize the way we use the phone.

Any equipment or system using a computer chip is digital– calculators wristwatches, digital thermometers, modems, one-touch cameras, coffee makers, cell phones, newer answering machines, automotive cruise control and electronic systems, copy machines, microwaves, computers (of course), printers, garage door openers, stereos, ATM machines, refrigerators, CD players, airline reservation and navigation systems, rice cookers, computerized exercycles, pacemakers, traffic lights, and much more.

In addition to digital-based equipment, there's software for data and information management, billing, payroll, word processing, and hundreds of other applications. Now imagine, if you can, all of this complex digital interplay taking place in an average day's work.

Workforce Trends: The Big Picture

The better grasp you have about how global events affect the digital workplace, the more prepared you'll be to meet the frontier's challenges. The world, by anyone's estimate, is truly a smaller and more connected place than anytime in history.

To learn where you're going, it's necessary for you to probe the current trends marking the end of the millennium and see where they are leading us. What segment of the population needs to retool its skills? Which industries are spurring new jobs and opportunities? What countries are leading the way with growing economies and the need for new products? Which segments of the economy are shrinking and growing? What skills will be needed to compete in the future?

Trends currently acting upon today's workplace come from several directions. Several of these have been identified by organizations such as the U.S. Department of Commerce and the Hudson Institute, an Indianapolis-based think tank committed to developing pragmatic, practical analyses.

Here's a realistic snapshot of the economic future, with trends affecting both countries and industries alike. If you remember one-tenth of what follows, you'll be the neighborhood digital guru.

The Big Emerging Markets (BEMs)

Which of tomorrow's big markets should you

pinpoint? The big emerging world markets in terms of GDP growth are Asian markets of China, Hong Kong, Taiwan, South Korea, and Indonesia. The next tier of growth includes Latin American markets, especially Argentina and Brazil. Mexico's short-term outlook is bleak, at least until their economic recovery plan solves their financial crisis. One thing, however, is clearly evident: All of these emerging markets will be vitally connected to the digital frontier.

One of the best examples is China, which has a population of over 1.2 billion people and is the most populous nation on earth. It is also the most coveted by companies hoping to gain a sales and marketing foothold in Asia.

While China's per capita income remains substandard when compared to developed countries, the penetration of consumer electronics is quite high. Almost 25% of the population owns a television, and upwards of 50% own telephones. If software and hardware companies can sell products to just one-fourth of the population, they will reach a market of 400 million customers.

While in the slow process of liberalizing trade, China continues to depend on heavy industry for much of its economy. However, the trend for greater high-tech trade with this giant is more promising than ever.

One interesting development in capturing the Chinese market is the building of a Chinese language word processor. The problem, of course, is that the Mandarin Chinese language incorporates thousands of characters. Hoping to answer the call is Apple Computer Inc. with its Apple Chinese Dictation Kit. This voice recognition program is capable of recognizing some 350,000 phrases. After an individual trains the system to recognize a particular voice, text can be processed five times as fast as with a keyboard.

Twelve markets represent the most energetic

developing economies. Currently, these twelve Big Emerging Markets (BEMs) account for almost 25% of total American exports.

The International Monetary Fund and U.S. Department of Commerce 12 major BEMs:

- China (12)

- Hong Kong (11)

- Taiwan (6)

- South Korea (9)

- Indonesia (30)

- Argentina (22)

- India (29)

- Brazil (18)

- Turkey (27)

- Poland (50)

- Mexico (2)

- South Africa (35)

Note: Ranking of each country for exports of US manufactured goods in 1993 is in parenthesis.

If you have any remaining doubt that major export markets are shifting as the 21st century approaches, then consider the following chart that compares U.S. exports to Japan, Europe, and BEM countries in 1993 contrasted to projections for the year 2000:

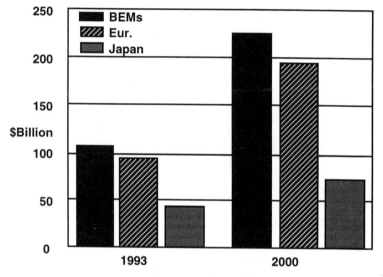

Source: Department of Commerce

The Service Share of the Economy Will Grow

The economic base continues to shift. But a loss of economy share in one sector doesn't mean that those jobs are lost forever. They simply move somewhere else. You can find many of those jobs in service industries, including telecommunications, computers, finance, and entertainment. The U.S. enjoys a huge trade surplus in services trade of $31 billion. Exports in this area will keep increasing.

The thought of moving to new service and digital-related industries is sure to come with some degree of trepidation. It helps if you recall that this process occurs periodically throughout history and always will, one prominent case in point being the shift from agriculture to manufacturing at the end of the 19th century.

Instead of hanging on to manufacturing jobs, why not capture the digital opportunities of tomorrow?

New Digital Jobs Demand a Higher Skill Level

What skills will you need to satisfy the digital job market? How do you retool existing skills to take advantage of the digital frontier opportunities? First, you'll need to be literate, which is clearly no problem for you since you're reading this. Then there is computer literacy. Uh oh, you say, but before you panic, read on.

Computers are commonplace in most school systems. Five and six year olds who inherit mom and dad's hand-me-down personal computers are navigating from the "C prompt" to various hard drives and sub directories, all the while playing with educational multimedia CD-ROM products as easily as their parents did with erector sets and Lincoln Logs. If children can learn computer skills, so can you.

The bottom line is that as the economy and work skills become more complex, the more necessary higher educational standards and training investments become for all of us. Fortunately, a fear of learning computer-related skills is countered with seminars, study-at-home and evening computer schools, and even personal computer trainers ready to help you succeed in the learning process.

When all is said and done, the best remedy for compu-phobics may be to plunge right in to the deep end of the pool. After all, the new digital frontier is much like the venerable telephone in that you can't be *hooked in* until you are first *hooked up*.

New Jobs by Women & Small Businesses

One major workplace trend is the emergence of women as new, successful business owners. Dun & Bradstreet Information Services reports a 42% increase in women-owned businesses from 1991-1994.

During this same three year span, the rate of employment grew more quickly in women-owned companies (11.6%) compared to the employment growth rate at all U.S. companies (5.3%). Perhaps most astounding of all is the fact that women-owned businesses actually hire more U.S. workers than do Fortune 500 companies globally.

With these businesses growing at a faster pace than the general overall economy, women-owned firms are successfully competing for a larger share of the marketplace. If you are looking for a job, it might be useful to know that employment among women-owned businesses grew at twice the rate of all United States businesses.

New jobs are also being created at a frantic pace from the small business sector of the economy. For example, just about half of the 3 million jobs created in 1995 were created by companies with fewer than 20 employees, states Dun & Bradstreet's *5000 Survey of Employment Expectations*. In contrast, firms with over 5,000 employees accounted for just 6% of the new jobs created in 1995.

There's another trend that's in the making, and it relates to the aging of the baby boom generation. The average workforce age will climb to 39 years by the year 2000. While these older workers are stable and experienced, it's a big plus if you are willing to consider relocation and a change of occupation.

Emerging Industries

Let's talk for a moment about the industries you'll encounter on the frontier. Each industry outpost contains its own unique mix of jobs in order to deliver its goods, services, and products. Is there any way to predict the occupational job mix of the future?

The answer is yes, according to *The Hudson Institute*, which predicts future changes by projecting an industry's occupational mix, and applying that to the structure of the economy as predicted in the year 2000.

Hudson Institute Study Prediction of Occupational Job Mix in the Year 2000:

"The results suggest that the job prospect for professional and technical, managerial, sales, and service jobs will far outstrip the opportunities in other fields.

In contrast to the average gain of about 25% across all occupational categories, the fastest growing fields– lawyers, scientists, and health professionals– will grow two to three times as fast. On the other hand, jobs as machine tenders, assemblers, miners, and farmers actually decline."

More specifically, here are some percentage increases predicted for digital-related occupations. Keep in mind that the digital frontier spreads across many industries– including legal, medical, marketing, and others.

Occupational Growth to the Year 2000

Occupation	%Growth
• Service Occupations (Management-related)	37%
• Marketing and Sales	39%
• Technicians	44%
• Health Diagnosing and Treating	53%
• Engineers	41%
• Computer and Mathematical Scientists	68%
• Writers, Artists, Entertainers	39%
• Lawyers	71%

In keeping with these percentages, low-skill jobs are obviously in decline, while new occupational growth areas demand higher skill levels. This may mean that the U.S. will continue to be the land of opportunity in the new century– but more so for those who are well educated, as opposed to those who in the past were simply lucky enough to be Americans.

Software and Information Services

Have you ever used a word processor? A check balancing program? Office software? A spreadsheet? The world's appetite for software is voracious and expanding. Packaged software accounts for a global market in excess of $77 billion. The U.S. is the world's leading software supplier and accounts for 75% of the overall business.

Software applications span the gamut of business needs, from generalized software to a variety of customized, industry-specific packages for publishing, distribution, law offices, and more.

Information services is yet another area where the U.S. leads in the exporting, usage, and creation of innovative networking and information solutions for the world market. With a 46% global share, the U.S. is the acknowledged expert in this thriving industry. Information services, for those who don't know, is an industry dedicated to managing, networking, or servicing information, much in the same way that we organize, process, and distribute the mass of paperwork generated in any office environment.

If you want to know where the information services industry is headed, the answer is to keep one eye on the government's developing policies, and to stay in touch with various industry associations which follow policy.

Although software and information services are distinct areas in this outpost, they sometimes converge. One new way in which these two areas are coming together is for the computer makeover– the hiring of consultants for a day or two to remake and customize an office computer system.

When *Independent Business Magazine*, in conjunction with Claris Corporation, sponsored a computer makeover contest, they received over 2,200 entries. The winners received a free information management makeover with a value of $5,000. The excerpt which follows describes the experience of one *Independent Business Magazine* makeover winner and illustrates how the right software and information management improves the way business is done.

Before and After Computer Makeover

"J World, a Newport, R.I.-based sailing school offers sailing courses throughout the United States. With a staff of 25, the company serves more than 1,000 customers each year and has yearly gross sales of $1 million.

For most of the company's 14 year history, J World used "computers that were as old as you could get and still call computers," says co-owner John Alofsin. The company's two aging PCs, which used unwieldy eight-inch floppy disks, were slow, cumbersome and severely limited in their abilities.

J World maintained separate files for each category of customers: one for students, another for buyers of the company's video, and so on. There was no way to target advertising according to a student's skill or familiarity with J World's courses or products.

All that changed after the office makeover. As part of J World's prize, small business consultants Bill Taube and Bruce Yogel, owners of Needham, MA-based Database Associates, Inc., installed and customized FileMaker Pro 2.1 for Windows and Macintosh– software that enables PCs and Macintosh computers to share information.

J World uses the new database to monitor the effectiveness of its ads, as well as to create targeted mailing lists. The firm tracks potential customers and sends personalized letters to sailing students. Even labels are printed with the system.

Computer Hardware and Peripherals

If you're not an electronic or computer junkie, you probably know someone who is. It's no surprise that the U.S. continues to lead in the computer equipment sector with a commanding 75% global market share.

The computer industry, while mature, changes rapidly. In terms of emerging new products and functionality, it has not yet hit its stride. There's a slow but sure trend toward interactive products that integrate music, voice, animation, music, and graphics. This new generation of products will revolutionize learning and entertainment.

In addition, there is the ever constant upgrading and technological advancement that is part of the product cycle which computer addicts live for. All in all, the outlook for the computer hardware industry is extremely promising.

On-line and Communication Services

This frontier outpost is bursting at the seams, in great part due to the growth of on-line services and the popularity of the Internet. America Online, one of the fastest growing services, is expected to increase its subscriber base from over 4 million in 1996 to about 5 million by 1997. The Internet, more accessible each day, is on its way to becoming an indispensable tool of industry and advertising.

And what about the more traditional mediums of broadcasting, cable, and film? Our steady companions for several years, all are jockeying for a front row seat in the digital frontier. Some even use the on-line services as a means of promoting their products.

All the major Hollywood studios offer interactive press kits and media packages that you can download into your computer. The press kit for Sylvester Stallone's *Judge Dredd* went so far as to include a playable action game. Typically, interactive press kits include movie credits, publicity photos, and theme music— all with the goal of getting users to shut down their computers, leave the safety of their cocoons, and venture out to the movie theater. It must be working.

You can bet your cyber dollar that these well established mediums will protect their market share by expanding into the frontier. A decade or so ago, media companies might have been content to concentrate on producing programming, but no longer.

Two examples of this digital expansion are media giants Fox and Disney. Rupert Murdoch, with his upstart Fox network, has forged an $8 billion world-wide media empire supported by an astonishing and spectacular (feel free to fill in any additional superlative of choice) satellite distribution system. With production in film, newsprint, and broadcast media, Murdoch's News Corp. is primed for merging its technologies into the interactive realm.

Entertainment leader Walt Disney Co., which draws on a wealth of products, is taking its products interactive. *The Lion King* movie, which was supported by the usual book and music products, was the first major Disney movie release to also enjoy an interactive CD-ROM.

Looking at the diversity and financial strength of these firms, it's easy to envision joint ventures and mergers between entertainment, software, and telecommunication companies. Meantime, these areas will provide the jobs and opportunities of a lifetime.

Creative Services

This fun frontier outpost is populated by highly creative people who are intent on inventing new forms of interactive entertainment, edutainment, games, training, music, and virtual reality-based products. Many of these new products will be delivered in *real-time* through the on-line medium.

Entertainment is one of the United States' largest exports, and an area where the U.S. has dominated for a long time. There's every reason to believe that new entertainment forms will attain the same viewership as traditional movies and TV. The boon in entertainment makes this an especially exciting time for writers, artists, and actors with a computer bent. If you've ever dreamed of being a power crazed mogul who runs a studio, multimedia might be your chance for total control.

With this creative freedom comes a valid concern for addressing the issue of electronic property rights–which just so happens to be an emerging area of the law. Best of all, you have the opportunity to experience new forms of learning and playing which are being invented every day. It could only happen out here on the frontier!

Advertising & Marketing

The Home Shopping Network and QVC are two great examples of the success of interactive marketing and advertising. Yes, this form of TV is interactive since viewers interactively dial their phone to place an order. These transactions are so commonplace as to be thought of as low-tech when actually they represent a very successful form of interactive marketing.

On-line infomercials already exist within the Prodigy, CompuServe, and America Online networks. The difference, however, is that on-line advertising encourages you to take an active part in the process. Instead of passively watching TV ads, new media advertising makes you part of the campaign, much like an actor. You simply click on interactive "hot spots" which link you to a sponsored area. From this area, you can search for more information, ask for brochures, and make a purchase via credit card.

Interactive public relations will play just as important a role. A large percentage of news stories already germinate from the pens of PR firms. Imagine what these very same prolific writers (for good or for bad) will do to the Internet.

Here's what you can expect from a complete on-line public relations and marketing campaign for a new product: Editorial reviews on the on-line services, a serialized Internet commercial for added buzz, World Wide Web promotions pointing to the product's Web page and linking it to related sites, coverage by on-line magazines and media, postings to Internet newsgroups, and even an on-line press party complete with special industry celebrities and guests.

Yet another area where the Internet's potential gleams bright is that of distribution. Already, many academic journals are routinely distributed through the Internet. You would be hard-pressed to find a form of distribution that is as fast, convenient, and economical.

In the new century, the distribution of ideas to hundreds of millions of people world-wide and *simultaneously* will be feasible, if not mind boggling—particularly when they can all respond, interact, or even vote if need be. The immediacy and impact of this ability for marketers and pollsters alike is extraordinary.

There is still a ways to go, and government will have a hand in shaping the on-line future. Since the government appears ready to ensure the security of data, the road will be cleared for allowing money to be exchanged over the Internet. With that happening, advertising, marketing, and distribution will play a major role in the digital frontier.

Virtual Reality

Every frontier has its furthest, most exotic outpost where only the most adventurous and courageous (perhaps foolhardy) explorers dare go. In the digital frontier, that place is not *Star Trek*, but virtual reality, or VR as it is known in the industry.

Sooner or later you'll venture to VR frontier land, if just to experience the fascinating and unusual entertainment applications. Virtual reality's most intriguing aspects, however, might lay outside the entertainment domain.

Because of virtual reality's sheer uniqueness and dynamic growth potential, it deserves a territory of its own in this book, if not the digital frontier. The film *Indecent Proposal*, which utilized virtual reality as a major plot point, let the audience step into Michael Douglas' shoes, or VR headset as the case may be. The allure, glamour, and seductiveness of this area will continue to grow as more applications abound.

For years, the defense industry has been using virtual reality as a training tool for pilots. The newest generation of F-22 fighter integrates virtual reality into the cockpit. A supersonic plane capable of flying beyond a pilot's normal skill level, it uses virtual reality display technology to help shield pilots from overload.

Virtual reality may be the ultimate tool for behaviorally re-conditioning anxiety disorder and phobias. The image-building capabilities of the computers that created the dinosaurs of *Jurassic Park* can also build entirely realistic (or non-realistic) work environments. Building virtual sets for TV shows will become commonplace. Commercials routinely merge images of fact and fantasy, giving credence to the question, "is it real, or is it virtual reality?"

How long will it be before terms like headtracking device, texture mapping, and double-handed controller are comprehended by the public? Like any new industry, techno-babble trickle down takes time. In this outpost, it will happen sooner than you think.

Retooling Skills for the Frontier

A digital world flickering with non-glare computer screens is nirvana to some, anathema to others. Those who refuse to patronize ATM machines or to use credit cards for fear of government or other abuse, need to be assured that their individual rights and freedoms are secure. Less concerned people already know the benefits that our digital frontier provides for them.

What you, as a frontier explorer need to contend

with is the gap between learning consumer and work-based technologies. Consumer-based technologies are designed for ease-of-use and must incorporate obvious benefits and economy of scale. Unfortunately, ease-of-use seems to be a dirty word for many work-based technologies. It's comforting to know that computers and software programs take the brunt of the jokes cycling through cyber space.

Computer Jokes for Computer Users

Shell to DOS...Come in DOS, do you copy?

Smash forehead on keyboard twice to continue...

*To err is human. It takes a computer to really *&@!.*$@! up.*

SENILE.COM found...Out of memory...

DOS Tip #3: C:\KNOCKNWD.COM

Read my chips: No new upgrades!

Cannot read hard disk: Schedule appointment with optometrist.

Backup not found: (A)bort (R)etry (C)rash Network

Software never develops bugs, just random features.

Press any key...no, no, no, NOT THAT ONE!

Take heart that computers are not the all-perfect devices that they are sometimes made out to be. After all, they were created and built by people, weren't they?

The point is, the only true obstacle to change comes from within. There is no single path to retool your skills or prepare for infopreneurial opportunities. The pathways are as many and varied as those of you who journey onto them.

Competition will ensure that workplace training grows along with the implementation of digital frontier technologies. The good news is that there's a lot of training to choose from.

Non-profit career planning centers provide counseling, assess skills, and offer on-the-job training and workshops.

Federal, state, and local governments offer a panoply of job training and job search programs. For example, the California Employment Development Department maintains a statewide computer network that matches applicants and job openings. They can also refer job seekers to the kind of advanced technology training and educational facilities that they need.

Public universities incorporate "new media" studies as part of the standard curriculum. The University of Virginia Publishing and Communications Program **(800-346-3882)** offers a three day seminar titled, *"Exploring the New Media: Migrating On-line from Print and CD-ROM, Business and Legal Issues."* Topics covered include everything from "Cyberlaw for Non-Lawyers" and "The Economics and Demographics of Internet Publication," to "Cyberspace Protection through Technology," and "The Future of Electronic Commerce on the Internet."

Professional training institutes are also migrating toward the digital frontier. The American Film

Institute, long dedicated to promoting film and television arts, offers advanced technology programs for animation, imaging, digital video, and multimedia.

Traveling road shows and seminars hop from state to state, and from hotel banquet room to hotel banquet room, extolling the business end of cyber space. The pragmatic, how-to topics found might include everything from how-to build a cyber store and use mailing lists, to a tutorial on using the Internet and its tools.

Computer fairs and local computer user groups across the country feature lectures, exhibits and seminars that run the gamut of the digital frontier.

At-home and videotape study programs cover most aspects of technology. Many software companies also offer videos showing how to use their applications.

The old adage that goes, "The harder you work, the luckier you get," still holds true. Retooling one's skills with these and many other training programs can only help better prepare you for the opportunities ahead.

If, by now you can amaze friends with your own brand of techno-babble, then it's time to leave the outpost and journey to the first outpost on the frontier. Good luck on your trip!

CHAPTER 2

SOFTWARE & INFORMATION SERVICES

"Do not worry about your difficulties in mathematics; I can assure you that mine are greater." *Albert Einstein*

Industry Snapshot

Welcome to the frontier's software and information services outpost. If you look around, you'll notice that this outpost encompasses more territory daily, with no end in sight.

The U.S. supplies about 75% of the world's software market. Much of this is controlled by software giants like Microsoft. Ongoing mergers are resulting in a few giant firms owning the lion's share of the market. Those software firms remaining will compete for hot niche markets desktop publishing, home and business information services, multimedia authoring, security, networking, and desktop video. Keep in mind that no one chapter could possibly cover every aspect of the entire software outpost. What follows are opportunity hot spots and emerging areas.

Service is the Name of the Game

Further, there is a whole new area dedicated not to technology per se, but to *servicing* technology. This includes the setting up of computer systems, servers, and networks, in addition to providing full training and field support.

The positions of Manager of Information Systems (MIS) and Network Administrator are critical to many businesses. For highly technical jobs like these, a degree in Computer Science and Engineering is practically *de rigueur*.

System complexity and the high cost of staff are causing more and more companies to out source facilities management tasks such as networking and data communications. A large amount of this work is being handled by servicing companies and consultants.

However, a skill and interest in any of the following occupations gives you the right to make the software and information services outpost home.

OCCUPATIONAL OPPORTUNITIES FOR:

- **Architects**

- **Artists**

- **Computer Security Specialists**

- **Database Consultants**

- **Data Communications Analysts**

- **Entrepreneurs**

- **Graphic Designers**

- **Multimedia Producers**

- **MIS & Network Administrators**

- **Photographers**

- **Software Developers & Engineers**

- **Systems Engineers**

- **Technicians**

- **Video Producers**

- **Writers**

In addition to the list above, there are opportunities for those of you who are educators, retailers, marketers, financial analysts, database managers, computer trainers, and exporters.

Whatever your specialty, you'll probably find it represented as one of the opportunity sectors discussed in this chapter, such as desktop publishing, business management and networking, multimedia authoring, and data security. If your area of expertise is not yet present, then there's plenty of room for developing and selling it. Explore the various opportunity sectors and see which appeals to you the most.

Before you go, stop in at Software Sammy's for a softwich, softdrink, and some softchat with the other pioneers. The techno-babble is pretty sedate there, except for the digital poker room where the programmers and networking types hang out. For a bit of a wackier time, visit the Toon Room, where the graphics and animation crowd gathers.

Desktop Publishing

Anyone interested in the software frontier should take the tour of the following publishing-related opportunities. With the advent of desktop publishing (DTP), artists, architects, graphics designers, and other creative types are adding value to their work. Graphics software, in fact, has advanced far beyond two-dimensional tools and low resolution images.

There is a demand for computer programmers and software developers who have their finger on the pulse of this market. Look for ways to service niche desktop publishing areas and you might find a winner.

√√ *Creation of Graphics Plug-In Tools*

When a software package is called "full-featured," that's usually a tip-off that it's cumbersome, full of difficult to learn commands, and takes hours to learn. The trend in finding an antidote for bloated software?: The use of plug-in tools. More and more of today's design tools use third party "plug-ins" to add enhanced functionality to a basic software package. Software developers who specialize in these add-ons can gain a huge following for their products.

Case Study–

Adobe Systems **(415-961-4400)**, is the maker of the popular image manipulation program called *Adobe Photoshop™*. The application, however, has so many different controls, that re-creating certain effects can be difficult to achieve. HSC Software **(805-566-6200)**, a California-based company, answered the call with *Kai's Power Tools®*, a powerful variety of plug-in filters and extensions that allow for quick, automated image manipulation.

Images can be rippled, sharpened, rotated, retouched, embossed, shadowed, or extruded, in only a matter of real-time seconds or minutes. The result?– professional-looking graphics and imaging that are accessible to almost everyone.

☞ NEW OPPORTUNITY

**Plug-Ins & Templates
for
Business Cards & Brochures**

Here's an entrepreneurial opportunity for software developers and graphic designers wanting to create a niche market product. The product?: Ready-made templates that small businesses can use to design and create their own customized cards and brochures.

Templates make a program conform (often using built-in macros) to what the user needs. The good news is that the built-in macros in computers and word processing programs will let you design templates with little or no prior programming background.

Small business owners and non-graphics professionals frightened off by complex page layout programs will appreciate templates that work with their word processor.

A small number of companies are offering brochure templates designed to work with two and four color pre-printed brochure paper. But there's a need for more professional looking, easy-to-use templates.

√ *Creation of Writing Templates*

Anyone who works with the built-in macros found in their word processor can build writing templates. Templates transform "kitchen sink" applications into customized ones. Word processing programs are designed to perform a wide variety of formatting tasks, but require a steep learning curve for the user who needs a specific format. Lawyers, for example, might need a specific format for briefs; academics require another format for journal publishing. Getting word processors to format according to accepted standards can be a lot like wrestling with a gorilla.

Case Study–

Scriptwriting Tools, from Minneapolis-based Morley & Associates **(800-464-7511)**, is an example of a writing template program that gives writers an edge. In addition to providing eleven templates for the popular *Microsoft® Word* program, *Scriptwriting Tools* also customizes *Word's* menus, provides keyboard shortcuts and glossary lists. Templates like this one offer other advantages as well. Users don't need to buy and learn a different word processor for each type of specialized writing. Templates simply adapt programs with which users are already familiar and comfortable. Plus, users won't fill up their hard drives with additional software.

☞ NEW OPPORTUNITY

Templates for Multimedia and Interactive Writing

Here's an opportunity for someone to build templates that are designed to give writers and multimedia developers a format for organizing their interactive scripts and ideas. A multimedia template that works with established word processors would help streamline and organize the process.

Such a template must simplify the initial design document. It should automatically create a rough prototype of the multimedia program by providing a list of all screens, graphics, photographs, sounds, and other elements used in the program. It might even provide automatic links between elements.

TRENDS 2000: Interactive Novels

The next generation of writers will broaden their work to include more than the written word, and may include sound and video clip "memories" of characters and places. The interactive novel will give the reader several simultaneous perspectives from which to experience the book, and will probably contain buttons that shift the action between characters, and storylines.

The finished products will run on a floppy disk, CD-ROM, or over the Internet. Ultimately, interactive novels may even allow users to "play" one of the characters and make choices that alter the story.

√√ *Electronic Publishing*

This form of publishing creates opportunities not just for established publishers, but for those who want a low cost publishing alternative. No wonder that booksellers are worried that one day in the not too distant future, you'll download your book onto your computer instead of buying it at their store. Right now, there are "electronic" books that can be bought and downloaded.

Of course, electronic books aren't for everyone. You don't get the same sharp, readable text on a computer that you do on paper; you can't carry a full-sized computer in your back pocket; and perhaps most important of all, you can't snuggle up with your computer in bed.

There are some things you can do with an electronic book, such as use powerful search and retrieval capabilities, and link interactive buttons to color images, sound, video, and other software programs. You can even take electronic notes without scribbling all over your copy.

Case Study–

The Voyager Company, **(914-591-5500)**, an

Irvington, New York-based multimedia producer and software developer, created *The Voyager Expanded Book Toolkit* software. The program makes it easy to publish electronic editions of previously existing works, or to publish new ones in full electronic form. After importing text from a word processing or layout program, the electronic publisher decides which areas to make interactive, such as the table of contents, indexes, or annotations.

Voyager has successfully published several of its own expanded books, and users of their software pay a small licensing fee. (We never said the digital frontier was free!)

Once an electronic book is created, it must be published by getting it on-line. New York-based BiblioBytes **(201-222-1600 & http://www.hauman@ bb.com)** is an electronic publisher that buys titles from print publishers and authors. The company has over 500 titles which it sells over the Internet.

TRENDS 2000: Publishing

While there is a demand for electronic publishing, the ultimate in publishing may come when you are able to have a book printed for you, right in your home.

Some in publishing predict that there will soon be consumer printers capable of printing typeset quality text and 4-color images while you wait. You'll choose the most comfortable type size, font style, even layout. Then, after you've chosen your preferred cover art from five different styles, your book will be printed and bound.

41

√√ *Clip Art for the Ages*

Clip art is finished, off-the-shelf art that can be used to lend a graphic touch to such things as newsletters, brochures, flyers, and ads. Creators of booklets and brochures of all types routinely use images that are pre-designed and ready to go. For them, clip art is the answer.

For you artists, photographers, videographers, and filmmakers, this area presents the golden opportunity to build a clip art library of your work and offer it for sale. In the past, clip art had the rap of being second tier, but that's changing because syndicated, well known artists are allowing their work to be sold this way.

Clip art falls into many categories. You'll find clip art of the masters, with digitized paintings of Van Gogh, Da Vinci, Michelangelo, and the like. Be aware that although the original image is in the public domain (no longer under copyright) the digitized image belongs to the company selling it, and cannot be altered. (More about this in Chapter 5.)

Photographic clip art is often sold by its category, such as cities, animals, nature, architecture, people, scenic sites, symbols, company logos, comic figures, and more.

With continuing advances in technologies that compress graphics and video images, companies like California-based Energy Productions **(818-508-1444)** even offer the ability to browse digital stock video through the Internet. Most importantly, this is your opportunity to get your work on-line.

☞ NEW OPPORTUNITY

Clip Art, Photography, and Video on CD-ROM

Photographers and videographers with a backlog of existing slides and video can categorize and sell them to stock photo houses, or they can have their images digitized and a CD-ROM mastered for sale. True, there is much clip art available, but there's always a need for niche market art.

One photographer who specializes in business photography is making a CD-ROM of business-related photos. The same can be accomplished for almost any type of photo.

Who uses clip art?– now-a-days almost everyone, including mom and pop Realtors who design their own flyers, corporate types who design newsletters, and advertising agencies who serve national accounts.

√√ *Animation and 3-D Tools*

For artists, designers, and multimedia developers who need to create figures, you'll find these tools indispensable. There's a growing demand for niche market modeling and rendering programs that make the artist's life easier, as well as put the power of artists and architects in the hands of mortals.

You'll be amazed at the eye-popping 3-D images being created by software. *KPT Bryce* is a program that guides you to effortlessly create detailed landscape images– mountains, clouds, water, and all. Yet another niche graphics product offers over 1,500 different edging effects for photographic images.

Some programs apply realistic-looking 3-D effects to 2-D images. Others provide a library of 3-D textures and models; advanced 3-D programs provide full modeling and rendering capabilities, allowing the user to change the perspective and lighting, and to place photo realistic skins over most objects. Of course, the easier and more intuitive these advanced graphics tools are, the better.

Animation and 3-D sculpted objects end up being used in multimedia programs, and thus would be ideal as plug-ins. There are even 3-D programs that draw the human form on the desktop– no previous art schooling necessary. So if you always wanted to create a super hero, these renderings of human forms can be posed, moved, and placed within 3-D environments.

Case Study–

Fractal Design Corporation **(408-688-8800)**, an Aptos, California-based software developer, offers a remarkable program called *Poser*™. The program makes human figure design and limited animation available to the average computer user.

Figures can even be posed in classical poses, such as "The Thinker," and "David," then rotated, moved, and stretched as desired. Human models should only be this accommodating.

☞ **NEW JOB AREA**

Web Site Designer and 3-D Internet Publisher

It seems that as soon as a new niche opens up, the frontier's developers answer the call with do-it-yourself software tools. For example, the proliferation of Web Sites has produced competing software packages to help you design your own Web Site on the World Wide Web. No doubt, artists and architects will step in and do the job for those who don't want to spend the time and effort to develop their own Web sites.

With the 3-D software now available, you'll even be able to build and publish customized 3-D environments on the Internet. This will give you the ability to create virtual stores and allow customers to literally take a walk through your space.

Many of the 3-D graphics programs allow for some form of animation, or movement of objects across the screen. Multimedia authoring programs will work with these images to create an experience combining interactivity, motion, and sound. For those who care, complete interactive shopping malls are just around the corner.

√ *Video on the Desktop*

Video editors, producers, and multimedia creators will need the sophistication that desktop video brings. Though it has been around for a few years, broadcast quality video editing and effects were always expensive and usually only found in the professional realm.

The processing power of today's hardware, however, makes high quality desktop video a reality at down-to-earth prices. Most systems combine an add-on board (hardware) with a software package.

Many of the new breed of computers, such as Apple's high end Power Macs, are designed to handle stereo input and output, and video (Composite-video and S-video) input and output. By corporate and video producer standards, true broadcast quality output still costs a bundle, but far less than just two or three years ago. Less powerful desktop video packages for home users offer pretty good quality for an affordable price.

Case Study–

Desktop video hardware/software packages are reaching the next generation of video and filmmakers. The non-linear editing systems made by companies such as Data Translation **(508-460-1600)**, TrueVision **(317-577-8788)**, Avid Technology **(508-640-6789)**, and Radius **(408-541-6100)** raise the standard to comprise 30 frames of video at 60 fields per second. That's the same number of fields used to deliver seamlessly smooth images on U.S. television sets.

But desktop video does much more, including digitizing and compressing video onto the hard drive, allowing for database management and logging of video clips, printing to video, editing of both audio and video, and building of transitions, titles, and special effects.

These systems are especially well suited to

multimedia producers who will output their final video product on computer. These complex packages range greatly in price- low end consumer packages cost from several hundred to several thousand dollars; broadcast quality packages range from a low of thousands of dollars to tens of thousands.

☞ NEW JOB AREA

Non-Linear Video Editor

In the late 60s and early 70s, news editors worked with film, cutting it by hand and splicing together news stories on flat-bed Moviolas. Then along came video, which forced film editors to re-learn editing on linear videotape editing systems. Soon, the massive, expensive betacam and one inch linear videotape editing systems will go the way of the Moviola.

Editors who make the transition to non-linear editing will have an edge. One hopes, of course, that new non-linear editors understand not just computers, but also the fundamentals and aesthetics of editing. Making the transition to non-linear editing will not be that hard for editors, but it will be essential as the digital frontier moves forward.

Business Management & Networking

Today, the business of managing business is like an industry unto itself. This sector of the software frontier continues to grow as quality, information management, networking, and productivity come to the forefront of business operations large and small. This is all good news for database consultants, networking specialists, client/server engineers, programmers, and managers of information systems. These are the hot areas as we enter the 21st century.

⩗ *Network Administration*

Wide Area Networks (WAN) and Local Area Networks (LAN) are shaping the overall business culture and environment of the '90s. Welcome to the land of hubs, workgroup servers, nodes, and packets. Increased networking especially provides opportunities for network administrators, network support staff, network hardware engineers, hardware technicians, and employees of Local Area Networking vendors.

If you have absolutely no interest in learning the foreign language that is networking, you might want to skip ahead. However, if it's music to your ears, read on.

☞ NEW JOB AREA

Net Technologist

Building networks that move data flawlessly and speedily is an art. A highly desirable job in coming years will be that of a net technologist, who troubleshoots the network and keeps a company up on the Internet.

Net technologists, like systems engineers, will need to know how to configure, install, and administer networking products, as well as manage system resources and optimize throughput. Those who complete their training as certified network engineers will have a leg up on this area.

Anywhere there are networks, from Internet Access Providers (Chapter 4) to corporate and government offices, there will be a growing need for Net Technologists.

And because networks, like most things, are subject to breakage, there will also be a need for qualified hardware technicians who understand how to troubleshoot hardware and software problems.

√√ *Middleware & Groupware*

Helping computers to interact harmoniously over a network has spawned a whole segment of software known as middleware. Software developers, engineers, programmers, trainers, writers, marketers, and salespeople will all benefit from this booming area.

For small networks, there are out-of-the-box middleware products available at computer chain stores. But the larger and more complex the network, the greater the need for middleware to bring compatibility to thousands of different computers and workstations.

The middleware market will grow by leaps and bounds, says International Data Corporation, a market researcher that predicts the segment to expand from a 1994 total of $50 million to a year 2000 total of over $1.5 billion.

Then there's groupware, which defines a class of software that is designed to let users share information over the network. If you have ever used your computer to route documents, schedule meetings, or use E-mail, then you've been using groupware. Groupware also includes software that enables fax, voice and data communications, videoconferencing, and more.

Case Study–

With sales of groupware expected to grow to over $4 billion by year 2000, this segment of the frontier is a hot one. Why else would IBM Corporation **(800-426-3333)** spend $3.5 billion to purchase Lotus Development **(800-343-5414)**, a $1 billion a year software company? Probably because Lotus, with its *Lotus Notes* program, has the potential to become the industry standard as a network information system.

In addition to Lotus, top groupware contenders include heavy-hitters Microsoft **(206-882-8080)**, Oracle Corporation **(800-633-0596)**, and Novell Inc. **(801-429-7000)**. And there are start-ups hoping to cash in on the groupware lottery, too.

TRENDS 2000:

Global Interactive Networks

Global interactive networks will send multimedia transmissions as easily and commonly as we make phone calls or send data via modem. Transactions for many goods and services will no longer require contact with, or be controlled from, a central authority.

These virtual information exchanges will transmit information 24 hours a day as an adaptive network for whomever is linked up. Adaptive networks pull together various resources which are controlled by discrete organizations in different locales. The resources adapt to meet the free-form needs of those utilizing the environment-rich information contained within.

Then, after an instantaneous transmission, the network returns to its previous disbanded state, where it awaits commands for new resources.

Valuable services, like real estate transactions, will be conducted primarily on-line. For example, a home buyer in Spain shops for a house in Chicago over phone lines and servers owned by different real estate and mortgage banking companies, and regulated by different governments.

This arrangement results in the buyer taking an interactive stroll through the property, checking on up-to-the-minute rates from different lenders, qualifying for the mortgage, and having a face-to-face chat with the seller or buyer.

In the words of John Morley and Stan Gelbert, authors of The Emerging Digital Future, *adaptive networks are "like an ant hill, where spontaneous decisions made by independent members are so in sync that the behavior of the group seems to be controlled by a single will."*

√√ Information & Database Management

You don't need to be a computer programmer to be a database management consultant. There will be employment opportunities for those who learn to use the tools and platforms necessary to develop and offer client/server database applications. There will also be opportunities galore for support specialists and office solution specialists who master the advanced functionality of existing applications and products.

Computer power gives business a myriad of ways to automate, analyze, sort, link, and search for information. Knowing what to do with information can be the difference between business success and failure.

For example, software that provides flat and relational databases give users practical tools that they can use to bring masses of information under control— just like the J-World sailing school that found new business opportunity by integrating its existing information on customers.

Software applications like Claris *FileMaker Pro*™ and Microsoft® *FoxPro* are cross-platform database solutions that work between IBM compatible PCs and Apple Macintosh computers. Database management programs deliver on the promise of greater productivity by allowing businesses to automate and keep track of inventory, write and print orders, and generate and record invoices— all in real-time.

In addition to database management, there are many other kinds of specialized information needs, including management of E-mail, address and phone books, calendars, project management, and scheduling.

Improved customer service is another useful by-product of database management software. Mailings and advertising can be targeted to various segments of the customer base. Businesses keep track of customers better, too. Business and software consultants using programs like *FileMaker Pro™* and *FoxPro* are able to build customized, automated solutions for business.

Many of these database programs don't require programming, but include customizable templates. Just choose the ones that are designed to work for a particular business application.

Case Study–

Meeting deadlines is critical for the news and print media. Because layout is such a time intensive process, many newspapers and magazines now use the automation power of database programs to bring their layouts and advertising under control.

Ad Layout System, a program by Managing Editor Software, Inc., is designed to automate advertising assembly page by page. The program keeps track of each ad, and interfaces with other ad databases.

Retail advertisers use similar automated database systems to help with high-volume ad production. Many objects can be linked together for use in an ad. Objects are moved into page layout programs, where pricing, ad copy, and pictures are automatically updated.

☞ NEW JOB AREA

Computer Makeover Consultant

In Los Angeles, a major radio station runs an advertisement extolling the benefits of a computer and database makeover. Minutes later, another ad sells the advantages of an all-natural breath cleanser. Is the need for computer help (or the need for fresh breath) really that great?

The need really is there, mostly because computers– despite all the hype– bear more resemblance to the early cars with manual transmissions than modern automatics. While improved operating systems like OS2, Windows '95, and Apple OS help, customized information management solutions are typically beyond the reach of the average user and require a consultant's assistance.

Do you know of a business that requires a makeover? The answer is yes, if: a business manually tracks inventory; a business uses index cards to list clients; a business uses the computer like a typewriter; a business is unable to maintain an updated customer, vendor, invoice, or inventory list; a business can't sort information or exchange it across the network. The list goes on and on.

Computer makeover consultants are skilled at analyzing a business, then working to design a database solution that automates existing, labor intensive processes. The intent is to help the company accomplish its goals faster and more efficiently, using the existing computer system. After software is designed and installed, makeover consultants spend time training the owners and employees to use the new system.

☞ NEW OPPORTUNITY

Database Management Templates and Stand-Alone Applications

One of the powerful features of a database management software like FileMaker Pro™ is that it's entirely customizable. Claris, maker of the program, publishes a book called the Claris Solutions Guide, which lists hundreds of companies having designed thousands of templates for almost any need or application.

As a developer of templates, you'll be able to target any niche area, such as advertising, aviation, construction pricing and bidding, customer and sales tracking, distribution, education, entertainment, finance, general business, real estate, publishing, and more.

Claris even offers developers a kit for producing stand-alone applications that don't require FileMaker Pro™ in order to run templates. (For more information about the kit call Claris (800-3CLARIS).

55

Multimedia Authoring

If the software frontier has one truly unique area, it is that of multimedia authoring software. In particular, computer programmers with a working knowledge of C, C++, and Visual Basic programming languages will be in demand to help create these authoring products. Game developers and educators will use them to create new content and entertainment forms.

A multimedia authoring program is the means by which audio, video, text, graphics, clip art and other graphics, animation, database information, and interactive elements are accessed, linked and combined to produce an overall product. Basically, it's the fundamental tool for shaping and formatting audio and visual information in new and unique ways.

Authorware developer Power Production Software **(310-937-4411 & http://www.pps@netcom.com)** creates applications that allow users to design their own customized multimedia programs, products, or presentations. The company's *Digital Box Office* gives multimedia developers a set of powerful tools accessed through a futuristic interface that makes producing complex multimedia easy. It even has 3-D virtual reality capability. Software programs like these will one day be as ubiquitous as word processing and spread sheet programs.

√√ *Presentation Tools Help Make the Sale*

Most businesses have advanced beyond the tired, show and tell slide presentation. The hottest tool on the executive desktop today is the new generation of multimedia presentation software. It lets executives create compelling presentations by combining text, motion, sound, charts, and video in a format that can be played on almost any desktop computer. These programs even allow for output of transparencies and slides.

For the corporate world, this is a big improvement. Many of these programs are designed to integrate with existing word processing and other software packages. Presentation software even allows for interactivity by creating interactive "hot spots" or buttons that the user can click on.

Case Study–

Astound, a multimedia presentation software by Gold Disk (**800-465-3375**), is a fine example of this executive tool. The program comes loaded with over 70 pre-designed templates. This means that users can choose from color and design styles that best match the message they're trying to get across.

Once a template has been chosen, it's easy to add text, graphics, charts, sound, even video. These various "events" are then coordinated by using a timeline. Interactive buttons can be placed on individual screens and then linked to other screens in the presentation.

For corporate types, the best part of multimedia presentations like *Astound* is that they are constructed in pieces and are easily modified. This means that a presentation initially designed for food technologists can be redesigned for restaurant critics by substituting a set of replacement titles, graphs, and screens as needed.

Final presentations can be saved onto floppy disks or sent over the network for distribution. A "player" can be created that doesn't allow any of the information to be altered– but only to be played.

☞ NEW OPPORTUNITY

Multimedia Resumes and Business Cards

If you own a video camera and know how to use graphics and multimedia authoring programs, then you have all you need to start a home business for the design and creation of multimedia resumes and business cards.

What are the advantages of an electronic resume? Let's step into the shoes of a job hunter for a moment. There you are, sending out resume after resume in search of a job. But you fear your resume looks like and sounds like all the rest. Besides, one page is hardly enough space in which to describe all your capabilities and vast past work experiences.

You're nervous about the interview process and end up going on interviews for jobs that are obviously not right for you. When the day is done, you're afraid that you're wasting time sending out cookie cutter resumes.

If only you had an multimedia resume. There on the main resume screen would be interactive buttons linking to education, experience, goals, job responsibilities, skills, even hobbies. Then there's that button that says "video clip," which plays a video where you manage to say something really important and impressive.

Another advantage is that the screener or viewer of your multimedia resume has the ability to choose what information to see and in which order to see it.

Best of all this resume fits on a floppy disk for easy mailing or is compact enough to be E-mailed without the hassle of wondering if the post office mangled your best efforts.

Multimedia resumes can even be designed with a "contact" button that effortlessly dials your phone and links you up with your dream job.

The inclusion of graphics and design work on a resume might require the additional space provided by a customized CD-ROM. (In that case, the resume would be more aptly called a ROMsume.)

Of course, these same design elements work for multimedia business cards (or business floppies as the case may be). A multimedia experience that contains video, graphics, text, and charts is ideal for describing services and products.

Viewers of these multimedia business cards can even save the information to their hard disk if they want.

√√ *Computer Based Training (CBT) and Sales*

Here's a great opportunity for instructional designers, trainers, educators, and others to add value to their work by transforming it into a multimedia project.

Once a project is authored and created, it is usually distributed via disk, CD-ROM, or on-line. Authoring programs differ in their capabilities. Some can track the end-user's responses and save these responses into a database. Users, for example, may take a test or survey that records their scores. Such capabilities are ideal for computer based training (CBT) applications. Other authoring programs offer excellent video and graphics capabilities that make them ideal for entertainment or edutainment.

Multimedia authoring can create compelling sales pitches designed to target specific audiences. The "pieces" of a multimedia sales pitch– consisting of video clips, interviews, and music– can be assembled literally on the spot.

For example, a salesperson might choose to target demographics of ages 18-24, causing one version of the program to play; however, if the demographics of ages 35-44 are chosen, then a different version would run.

Case Study–

One of the most widely used multimedia authoring programs is *Director*. Macromedia **(800-288-4797)**, a San Francisco-based company and maker of *Director*, has developed a number of other ancillary multimedia tools. These include programs for font building, 3-D modeling, and video and sound editing. All of these products are packaged together into what is called *Director Multimedia Studio*.

It really is akin to a complete multimedia studio. All the tools needed to create, synchronize, and integrate production components are here. Those using *Director* need to learn its internal programming language to create professional CBT multimedia products.

☞ NEW OPPORTUNITY

Interactive Catalogs & Reference on CD-ROM

One area that is just being tapped is the creation of multimedia authoring programs dedicated to organizing massive product databases and complex project management procedures. Corporations can clearly benefit by cataloging information on to interactive, multimedia CD-ROMs. The experience of BP Oil illustrates the advantages of interactive cataloging.

BP Oil decided to use interactive cataloging to simplify and organize the contents of its essential project management information. What once filled a four-foot bookshelf now fits onto a single CD-ROM disk. The disk contains a collection of information covering all aspects of project management, including the best and most successful projects over a period of many years.

Accessing the CD-ROM via Windows and BP Oil's proprietary software electronically links all text and documents in the library. Users have the capability to instantly jump to any word, reference, or document on the CD-ROM by pointing and clicking with a mouse.

To make their library of information easy to use, the program allows users to place bookmarks in frequently used sections, print out forms, checklists, or procedures, and even get context sensitive help.

Most important is the way the checklists link up with the reference library. Many checklist activities link to guidance and warning references. If a warning reference is chosen, the user is referred to appropriate sections describing precautions. By linking up with internal documents, users can even take advantage of lessons learned from past mistakes.

The end result is more than a step-by-step interactive checklist of project management activities. With the CD-ROM library, Project managers can plan and organize projects by tailoring the checklist to a specific project. Members of the project team can prepare initial plans. Senior management can establish guidelines and standards for use throughout the company, and ensure the effective management of large capital projects. Contractor performance can be measured and monitored. Even new people involved in project management can use the CD-ROM as a training tool.

Data Security

Hackers, computer viruses, and computer banking fraud have sparked valid concerns over the security of data. The growth of the Internet makes this area all the more critical.

As a result, computer security specialists have become hot job prospects who are sought after within the banking industry, the corporate world, and the government.

☞ NEW JOB AREA

Cyber Cop

You're a cyber security guard, but you don't necessarily carry a gun or a badge. You're probably a hired hand, a computer programming hot shot like Tstutomo Shimomura, the security expert who succeeded at finding the elusive computer hacker Kevin Mitnick.

Security is an issue for corporations that depend on networking of information. Programmers creating algorithms for data security will find employment either as consultants or as employees of software companies creating security applications. It's also important to the freedom of speech (E-mail included) advocates who contend that encrypted on-line transmissions should be free of all government access.

And, as Internet commerce grows, there will be a need for cyber force officers of the law who possess the computer know-how necessary to fight Internet fraud.

√ *Digital Certification and Security*

Who would have thought that E-mail would become such a ubiquitous service that it would spawn J(unk)-mail? None-the-less it has happened. As a result, even the U.S. Postal Service is getting into the act, promising to establish a plan for digital E-mail letter certification.

Plans such as these could serve to authenticate that the E-mail you get is absolutely from the person who sent it. Still, you need to block out all that J-mail from cluttering up your mailbox.

Case Study—

Encryption technology developers RSA Data Security **(415-595-8782)** and CommerceNet **(415-688-4347 & info@commerce.net)** are working to secure Internet commerce by ensuring the identities and access authorizations of credit card users. There are several other on-line cash and credit systems representing major banking institutions which are vying for acceptance.

There's also PGP, a free encryption shareware which is already available over the Internet. PGP is based on the concept of dual encryption. In essence, this means that both parties have a "key" or password to unlock data transmissions. However, it's not infallible and there are obstacles to authenticity that need to be overcome— such as protecting against phony or counterfeit keys that have someone else's name on them.

The answer, according to the Postal Service, would be to encode digital verification into keys so that any alteration would be detectable. In the meantime, other cyber security experts will devise encryption systems for this nascent area of the frontier.

CHAPTER 3

HARDWARE

"Every moment of life is an opportunity and the greatest opportunity is to know the value of opportunity." *Inayat Kahn*

Industry Snapshot

You've just landed on the hardware outpost of the frontier. Things are boom or bust out here, despite the U.S. global market share of 75%. Computer equipment is solidly entrenched, but price cutting and new chip technology keeps the industry topsy-turvy.

To remain competitive in the expanding market of the '90s, computer equipment firms will keep their work force trim and lean, and be ready to adapt and restructure if necessary. The move towards computer standardization will place a premium on value, quality, and price, as opposed to brand name loyalty.

I Want My Extra Functionality

In addition to computers, there are many emerging products and technologies that promise to make the digital frontier more useful, friendly, and practical–including personal digital assistants (PDA), pen operating devices and systems, voice technologies, digital cameras, virtual reality systems, and super high density CD-ROMs.

These and other emerging hardware technologies are good news for those of you involved in product management and marketing. Since many of these new products are linked to software, software engineers are likely to find solid employment opportunities.

Anyone already trained and employed in the following areas should consider setting up shop in the hardware outpost.

OCCUPATIONAL OPPORTUNITIES FOR:

- **Electronics Engineers**

- **Computer Chip Engineers**

- **Computer Programmers**

- **Computer Repair Technicians**

- **Entrepreneurs**

- **Marketing Staff**

- **Mail Order & Retail Outlets**

- **Public Relations**

- **Product Design and Management**

- **Software Engineers**

- **Systems Engineers and Analysts**

- **Multimedia Designer/Producers**

- **Publishers**

- **Technical Writers**

As you navigate through the hardware outpost, you might want to visit the Hip 'n Hype Grill where the marketers hang out. If you're scientifically inclined, go to the All Chips Cafe. (Mention this book and get one math problem worked out for free. Limit one problem per meal.)

CD ROM Industry

CD-ROM players have become a staple of home and business computing. The player is the engine that runs CD-ROM discs. The CD-ROM player is like a record player, except a record player only plays music. CD-ROM discs contain music, film, video, and games, and are a major segment of this market.

As a side note, a new standard for videodiscs means that your venerable VCR will eventually be replaced by a higher quality videodisc player. This new standard will offer greater data storage capacity, too. So keep an eye on this area.

Whether discs contain music, reference materials,

video, or games, CD-ROMs are big business for all involved. Where does the money go when you peel off a $20 bill for the latest CD-ROM product? The following graphic explains who gets how much in this industry, which is based on the economics of the recording and publishing industry.

Where Do CD-ROM Dollars Go?

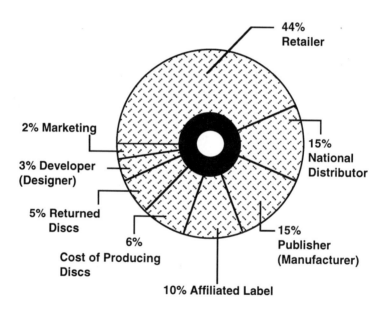

Note: Business agreements and market factors may effect percentages

Source: "The Joy of Licensing: The Multimedia Lawyer's Cookbook" by Robert Steinberg and Alan Sege.

☞ NEW OPPORTUNITY

CD-ROM Mastering

If you want to get in the business of mastering your own CD-ROMS, or doing it for someone else, there has never been a better time. This is an ideal opportunity for multimedia producers and service bureaus. It might even make an ideal home business.

Several CD-ROM recorders (CD-R) and their software components sell in the $1,000 to $2,000 range. For that price you can master a multimedia CD-ROM or archive and store important data for safe keeping.

If you only have to duplicate a small number of discs for testing, having a CD-R saves over duplication plants that usually ask for a minimum order of several hundred discs. Depending on the software, you can burn in various data types, video, and audio files. Most quad speed CD-R software can master a disc in about twenty-five minutes.

*Companies like JVC (**714-261-1292**), Sony (**603-891-4330**), Pinnacle Micro (**800-553-7070**), and several others are competing in the CD-R arena. How can you use this hardware to create new jobs and opportunities?*

*Planet Three Multimedia (**714-589-0455**), a Rancho Santa Margarita, California-based* *multimedia producer purchased a CD-ROM recorder and is using the new capability in several ways. First, the firm uses the recorder to archive important data. The company also masters a small number of its own multimedia CD-ROMs for beta testing and marketing purposes. Finally, the company uses CD-R to save space and help organize by category hundreds of different photographs and graphic images onto CD-ROM. The company plans on offering various collections for sale as stock photography via direct mail.*

√√ *Hybrid CD-ROMs Tap into Interactivity*

While we wait for true interactive television (which requires a broadband network), developers have come up with a dazzling simulation of the experience. The feat is accomplished by linking CD-ROM discs with on-line services.

All in all, this new format will open a world of opportunity for developers, publishers, and on-line services. There's a need for computer programmers who know programming languages like C++ and script X-commands that link the disc to the on-line service.

Basically, here's how hybrid CD-ROM discs work. The discs are embedded with both multimedia files and a communications link to an on-line service. After linking up via phone and modem, the disc accesses and updates local on-line databases.

To simulate interactivity in a visual environment, the CD-ROM disc utilizes the multimedia graphics and background information stored on it as the phone line transmits the user's actions, updates the hard disk, and ultimately plays on the output device.

The bottom line?: Financial, reference, educational, and entertainment CD-ROM titles that can gain access to the latest available information, such as stock quotes, new exhibits at the Smithsonian, book and catalog updates, and cuts from *Sting's* new music CD.

Even more intriguing are the networking opportunities created by hybrids. You might choose to create a virtual community of multiple game-players who compete on-line. Educators can organize students from around the country to participate in a virtual class room. Don't forget the home shopping possibilities, which will capture a networked audience having similar interests.

Case Study–

If you're involved in marketing or advertising, you can use hybrid CD-ROMS to give your business an interactive edge. Blockbuster Entertainment Group **(800-827-4955)**, America Online **(703-448-8700)**, and Ventana Media **(http://www.vmedia)** all did it and so can you. The thumbnail sketches that follow tell how.

Blockbuster Video's *Guide to Movies and Videos* brings users the latest reviews and movie publicity shots. Blockbuster's hybrid system only searches for those updates not already on the hard drive, and it does so transparently, in the background.

Through America Online, users of the hybrid *2Market* can shop for products from twenty-five virtual stores. Users can search for exactly the items they need, then place their order electronically.

Ventana Media publishes computer books with the ability to update their information. The books come with a hybrid CD-ROM disc. The disc actually links to a site on the Internet from which users can browse an electronic version of their book and get the latest updates. The publisher is licensing this technology to others.

Peripherals

The popularity of peripherals and accessories has caused them to sprout like weeds throughout the frontier. Think about it– have you ever thought about owning a Personal Digital Assistant (PDA), low-cost color printer, or a digital camera?

For every peripheral and accessory, there's an untapped opportunity. Here are a few that populate the frontier.

Peripherals, how many ways do I love thee?

3-D stereoscopic glasses

Blueprint scanners

Business card readers

Cables, cables, cables

Carpal tunnel syndrome wrist pads

CD-ROM players and changers

CD-ROM recorders

CD-Interactive

Cellular telephones

Color laser printers

Computer security locking systems

Computer speakers

Computer video-cams

Desktop label printers

Desktop paper scanners

Digital cameras

Ergonomic computer stations

External hard drives

Fax machines

Filmstrip scanners

Full screen monitors

Headphones, microphones, and MIDI

Infrared remote printing devices

Keyboard foot control pedals

Keyboard storage systems

Large screen presentation projectors

Low-cost color printers

Multiple plug and switching devices

Network adapters

Notebook batteries and chargers

Notebook and sub-notebook computers

Personal digital assistants

Phone-fax-answering machine switchers

Pocket modems

Point pads, graphics tablets, and joy sticks

Portable floppy drives

Portable printers

Scanners

Tape drives

Uninterruptible Power Supply (UPS)

Video, graphics, and TV plug-in cards

Virtual reality headsets

The above list points out abundant job opportunities in the areas of product design, product management, and marketing. Remember, this area is so huge that it would be impossible to cover each peripheral in detail. To get an idea of where to find more hardware opportunities, you'll want to go to the Networking Resource Guide.

Meanwhile, check out the following sectors in this outpost.

√√ *Digital Dollar Smart Cards*

A whole new industry is hoping to cash in on the shift in the way we will use money in the near future.

If those involved are correct, then electronic money is right around the corner.

What jobs and opportunities will result from this new technology? As with the credit and banking industries, there will be a need for in-house departments or third party companies to process and service all transactions. In turn, the volume of transactions and the breadth of access will place increased demands on computer security and system administration.

A cashless society will be made possible by credit card sized smart cards that will be used as cash to pay for everything from parking meters, groceries, and restaurant bills to video game usage and charges on the Internet. Even fast food would be available by smart card because the merchant fee associated with credit cards would be unnecessary for low cost transactions.

You'll transfer money into your smart card by using the phone. It's that simple. Plus, the cards will even be smart enough for world-wide use by converting to different currency exchange rates. The smart card's brains are located in a computer chip. But it will take the impetus of the banking and credit industry to prime the pump.

Case Study–

A coalition between BankAmerica and MasterCard International is promoting electronic money that uses the Netsite Commerce Server software (**800-NET-SITE**) from Netscape Communications. Yet another possible system, which is a variation on the traveler's check, uses disposable money cards that can be bought in various denominations.

One company, British based Mondex, is testing out its smart card in England, with plans to expand to Hong Kong, Canada, and other countries in the near future. Regional banks will buy franchises to use the Mondex smart card system and technology.

√√ *LCD Projectors Shine a Light on Business*

Can you guess how many corporate meetings are held each week? You better sit down, because according to some research firms, if you guessed less than 40 million, you underestimated the number of execs and middle managers mired in meetings. That's a lot of eyes straining to see blurry whiteboards, transparencies, and slides.

Do you sense a great sales and marketing opportunity here? That opportunity amounts to more than $1 billion. That's the amount of retail sales racked up by LCD projectors in 1994. Here's a peripheral that will certainly continue to increase its sales in the years ahead. A sophisticated multimedia presentation that outclasses slide shows by a mile is as easy as plugging a laptop into an LCD projector.

LCD projectors use active-matrix technology and are capable of playing full multimedia presentations. LCD projectors produce graphics and video images of up to 10 feet by 6 feet. Generally, projectors offer uniform brightness and good color intensity when compared to LCD panels.

Case Study–

This peripheral niche area is being pursued by several major competitors. Well known heavyweights like 3M Visual Systems **(800-328-1371)**, NEC **(214-751-7246)**, Sanyo Fisher **(310-605-6527)**, Polaroid **(617-386-2000)**, and Sharp **(201-529-8731)** have entered the market. But so have some lesser household names such as Apollo Presentation Products **(800-777-3750)**, Sayett **(716-264-9250)**, Proxima **(619-457-5500)**, and In

Focus Systems (**503-685-8888**), to name a few. For San Diego-based Proxima, the success of its LCD panels and projectors has caused them to move away from their beginnings as a provider of computer accessories.

Good jobs and opportunities are found among the marketing and sales staff of these companies. After all, these are the people whose efforts make or break specialized peripherals costing thousands of dollars.

√√ *Cellular Phones and Paging Devices*

In 1995, a record number of 14 new telephone area codes were added in North America. There are over 20 million Americans brandishing cellular phones. To that ever increasing total, add fax lines, pagers, and other mobile devices, and you're gobbling up about 8,000 new telephone numbers a day.

Even if you aren't lucky enough to own a phone company, you can still find opportunities here in the manufacturing and retailing of cellular phones.

Cellular phones are no longer the status symbols of the '80s. Cell phones have become ubiquitous, representing the staple of communications in many third world countries. In Taiwan, for example, where telecommunications have always been under government control, private firms are finally being allowed to provide cellular service.

In addition to cellular phones, wireless networks keep business people electronically dialed in with sky-paging systems, E-mail, and faxes. To keep pace with these advances, hotels are wiring up rooms with enough computers, printers, and fax machines to keep computer installers and technicians busy for years.

Case Study–
With AT&T's (**800-242-6005**) $12.6 billion acquisition

of McCaw Cellular Communications **(206-803-4000)** in 1994, it instantly became allied with the leading provider of cellular phones in the United States. More importantly, AT&T will be positioned to provide wireless service to its more than 80 million plus customers.

☞ NEW OPPORTUNITY

Specialized Cellular Products

*Hewlett Packard **(800-752-0900)** was California's second highest-rated company in 1994 with a $31.5 billion value (Intel **(408-765-8080)** was first with $39.3 billion). With such deep pockets, Hewlett Packard is able to develop new specialized uses for cellular technology.*

One example of such a product is PalmVue, a palm-sized wireless computer capable of monitoring a patient's heart rate, blood pressure, electrocardiogram, and other vital signs. Developed by HP's medical products group, PalmVue lets doctors diagnose patients more quickly so that treatment can start immediately.

The system is expected to help cut costs for HMOs and hospitals. And it means that even if your doctor is on the golf course, you won't have to wait until he or she finishes playing before you can get treatment!

Semiconductor Industry

The expansion of the semiconductor industry means new jobs and opportunities for programmers, chip designers, and engineers. Because chip makers are investing heavily in new equipment, it's a good time for machinery designers and others involved in manufacturing equipment that makes semiconductors.

Historically, the semiconductor industry is one of the most volatile sectors of the digital realm and subject to boom or bust. The semiconductor industry's worldwide revenues, which leveled off at $50 billion from 1988 to 1990, doubled to almost $100 billion by 1994. According to Semiconductor Industry Association projections, worldwide revenue is expected to double to over $200 billion by the year 2000. That number may actually be conservative. Consider: The percentage of chip capacity being used in factories reached an all-time high of 95% in 1994. In case you're wondering what's breathing life into this industry, it's a whole new breed of semiconductor dependent products.

√√ *Where to find the Chips*

Product managers and designers, computer chip engineers, computer programmers, and software engineers will appreciate that the semiconductor industry is no longer dependent on a few computer products as in the past. Remember the broad spectrum of products using chips that were mentioned in Chapter 1? Well, five years from now, a new wave of chip laden products will make their way into our lives.

Cutting edge digital products include high-definition TV, virtual reality video games, computer voice mail systems, video telephones, high speed ISDN phone lines, pocket computers, credit-card sized computer plug-in modules, home automation, two-way pager systems, and other wireless devices. Perhaps the most awaited product of all is the set-top hybrid: A universal device that's a computer, phone, and television all in one and connected to a high-speed broadband network.

Case Study–

One company making chips for specialized digital products is LSI Logic **(415-428-4700)**. With over 3,700 employees and earnings of over $900 million in 1994, this Silicon Valley-based company supplies chips for RCA's home satellite receiver. It also makes core chips for Sony's video game, PlayStation. In the future, the company hopes to be a major supplier of chips for video disc players as they begin to supplant the VCR.

Nexgen **(408-435-0202)**, also based in Silicon Valley, manufactures clone processor chips for use in computers. The company, with over 130 employees, invested millions in developing its clone, and believes that the computer industry's price-cutting practices will fuel the need for low-cost processors.

Two California start-up chip companies, Mountain View-based Chromatic Research Inc. **(415-254-5800)**and Sunnyvale-based MicroUnity Systems Engineering **(408-734-8100)**, are developing a new generation of specialized multimedia chips called media processors. A single media processor chip will be capable of processing 3-D animation, sound, and video.

☞ **NEW OPPORTUNITY**

PCMCIA Cards

Just when you thought acronyms were

getting shorter, something like *PCMCIA* comes along. It's the new credit-card sized slot for computer plug-in cards and wireless modems. (You won't be expected to remember that *PCMCIA* stands for Personal Computer Memory Card International Association!)

PCMCIA cards, shortened to the name *PC Cards*, bring increased functionality to laptop computers without adding all the weight and bulk. There are PC cards that let you instantly add a modem, more memory, or networking capability.

Full-sized computers can be fitted with sound cards to bring *CD-ROM* and other multimedia products to life with high fidelity sound. Since laptops offer limited internal real estate for adding cards, stereo sound is available through PC sound cards.

Many sound boards and PC cards utilize a specialized *DSP* (digital signal processing) chip to speed up sound processing, plus provide functionality used in the new digital answering machines. The chips provide smart features such as voice announcement, personal directories, and multiple mailboxes.

TRENDS 2000:

ID Chips

The day will come when children may carry tiny, implantable computer chips under their skin as a form of identification.

Of course, there are privacy hurdles to overcome, but the precedent has been set in the animal world.

Consider that currently, such chips are being implanted in pets as a way to keep vital information including the owner's name, phone, and address.

In several cities, the ASPCA is using such a system and has bought the devices that will read the chip's contents. The chips are passive in that they require no batteries and can be read from a foot away. For those who find implants objectionable, the chips can be placed in necklaces, bracelets, or sneakers.

Currently, the Australian wool industry and Yamaha motorcycles have used ID chips to track bales and motorcycles, respectively. The benefit of safeguarding against theft is sure to make ID chips useful to other businesses.

☞ NEW OPPORTUNITY

Digital Video

The desktop, as you saw in Chapter 2, is going digital video in a big way. But while that chapter looked at the software side, here's a look at the chip-based hardware side.

For video to be captured on to a computer's hard disk, it needs to be compressed for efficient storage, as well as accelerated for quality playback and recording. Basically, lower quality video capture boards can cost from a few hundred to a few thousand dollars, while high end professional boards can cost several thousands of dollars.

MPEG (Motion Pictures Experts Group) is an accepted standard for the compression of full motion video and audio. Computer makers even offer MPEG video decompression boards that work for CD-ROM capable laptops.

A good example of how many of the frontier technologies we've been exploring converge to work in concert is PIX Productions (714-250-1749), a Costa Mesa, California-based interactive training and corporate video producer. After shooting a video, PIX uses multimedia software to author an interactive program. Next, PIX masters the program onto a CD-ROM disc, using a CD-R recorder.

The CD-ROM is delivered to PIX's client, who plays the presentation on a CD-ROM laptop containing an MPEG card. If the audience is too large for screening on a laptop, the computer is simply plugged into an LCD projector.

Video chips and accelerators will continue to grow in importance as more and more computers offer out-of-the-box video capture capability or MPEG chips to decode video. As mentioned earlier, many Apple Macintosh

Power PC computers already ship with a basic level of audio-video capability built-in.

Storage

If you were one of those early digital pioneers who were lucky enough (or *un*lucky enough) to have owned a computer circa 1980, you may remember that early personal computers did not come standard with hard disk storage. They only had floppy disk storage. Back then, a megabyte seemed infinitely large. A gigabyte (1,000 megabytes) was unheard of, unless maybe you were a sci-fi enthusiast. Today, a gigabyte of storage is routine, and a terabyte (1,000 gigabytes) or petabyte (1,000 terabytes) may not be too far behind.

The problem is that multimedia, video, and graphics applications and files consume huge amounts of disk space. But out here in the storage sector of the digital frontier, it's a wonderful problem to have. You'll find the same kinds of plentiful jobs and opportunities in the storage sector that you'll find elsewhere in the hardware outpost.

So have a look around, and while you're visiting, check out *Trends 2000: Nanotechnology* to learn about a really, really small area of study where the future is going to be really, really big.

√√ *Portable, Removable Storage*

Change in the computer industry only means a constant stream of new and better products for engineers to design and salespeople to sell. So it is with storage. Large capacity hard drives will continue to be placed in computers. It's the floppy drive that's in danger of becoming obsolete. It will most likely be replaced by one of the new high density removable media drives being built.

The amount of storage that can be placed on these removable drives will make them ideal for archiving or backing up large graphics or multimedia files. You'll also gain an incredible amount of flexibility.

Suppose you've been at the office working on a large multimedia presentation. You'd like to tweak it to perfection on your laptop computer over the weekend. But the file is too large to fit in your laptop's hard drive. No problem. You take the high density removable drive and disk home with you. Better yet, you have a removable drive plugged into your laptop, so all you need to do is plop the high density disk into your briefcase pocket and you're home free.

Case Study–

Utah-based Iomega Corporation **(800-777-6654)** is helping to transform closet-sized removable storage devices into warehouse-sized ones. The company's new drive uses a 3.5-inch removable media capable of storing 100 megabytes and uses inexpensive individual cartridges.

Some companies are even replacing the traditional floppy drives with high density removable drives. Uh oh, you're thinking: "What am I supposed to do with all my existing 3.5-inch floppies? Use them as coffee table coasters?" Save those 3.5-inch floppies, because the new high density removable drives will most likely accommodate them.

Iomega Corporation also manufactures a super high speed 1 gigabyte drive with a removable cartridge. This high density cartridge will be ideal for archiving or working on desktop multimedia and video projects.

TRENDS 2000: Nanotechnology

Nanotechnology is the science of making machines out of the tiniest things around: atoms. The machines they could build would be small enough to repair damaged cells, or build a memory storage device that would use chemistry to alter molecules.

As amazing as it seems, mathematician Leonard Adleman used a molecular, DNA-based computer to perform calculations hundreds of times faster than our fastest supercomputers. This research, and that of centers like the Xerox Palo Alto Research Center (Parc), will one day create a storage medium billions of times more dense than what exists today.

Nanothinc, a California-based corporation ***(http://www.nanothinc.com)***, *is a Web-zine dedicated to covering all research and commerce based on nanotechnology. The experts, according to Wired, say this:*

When Will Nanotechnology Happen?

	Molecular Assembler	Nano-computer	Cell Repair	Commercial Product	Nanotech Law
R. Birge	2005	2040	2030	2002	1998
D. Brenner	2025	2040	2035	2000	2036
K. Drexler	2015	2017	2018	2015	2015
J. S. Hall	2010	2010	2050	2005	1995
R. Smalley	2000	2100	2010	2000	2000
Bottom Line	2011	2041	2029	2004	2009

Source: Wired Magazine

√√ *Hard Drives for Digital Video*

The demand for faster and better mega storage will only mean more opportunities in this sector of the frontier. That's because specialized, super fast, super capacity hard drives are needed for digital video, and video sucks up disk space faster than a Hoover sucks up dirt. Even tech guys can appreciate that.

Now for the more detailed explanation. Full motion video plays at 30 frames per second. Any slower and you get a blurry, jerky motion. However, single frame of video comprises a dense, graphic image occupying close to 1 megabyte of disk space.

To achieve full motion video from a computer requires the hard drive to pump out a full 30 frames of video to the monitor each second. That equates into 30 megabytes of disk space for each *second* of video! Fortunately, the video images are compressed into smaller sizes on the hard drive. They're still huge, and only recently have hard drives been designed to work with digital video so that frames are only rarely "dropped" or missed.

Case Study–

Seagate Technology **(408-438-6550)**, a California-based Fortune 500 company, is a recognized leader in the designing, manufacturing, and marketing of storage technologies. Seagate is not alone, as the field for manufacturers includes Micropolis **(818-709-3300)**, Conner Peripherals **(408-456-4500)**, and Quantum Corporation **(408-894-4000)**, as well as Hewlett Packard and IBM.

Manufacturers are packing up to 9 gigabytes of storage onto single disk drives. These drives can also be linked together to add as much storage as is needed.

Transmission

If you're a product or network engineer who is interested in the hardware side of networking, pay close attention to the following emerging trends and opportunities. One thing is certain, this area is rapidly expanding throughout the frontier.

Communications requires equipment, and lots of it. According to the Electronics Industries Association, manufacturers in the United States shipped about $64 billion of communications equipment in 1995. That's almost a 25% increase over the previous year. What's happening? The global corporate community is getting hooked up, flexing its technology, and trying hard to find new ways to do business.

New and advanced transmission equipment allows global and local companies to transmit and share video, voice, and data over high speed networks far faster than is possible over analog phone lines.

This equipment also makes working at home possible for employees in certain businesses. For example, the real estate arm of Prudential recognizes this, and is taking steps to redesign the more compact, networked real estate broker office of the future.

In other cases, communications equipment makes businesses more productive, automated, and efficient. For example, did you ever wonder how the book superstores handle inventories of 50,000 or more different books? The networked bookstore links its inventory to sales. When the inventory of any book shrinks to a predetermined level, a restocking order is automatically triggered.

√√ *Wired Communications*

If you're reading this, you probably have somewhat

of a technical background. But even if you don't, hang in there. We'll try to keep it simple by setting the stage with a few words about two of the most basic and established transmission mediums: Copper and fiber-optic cable. Both will be around for a long time, which means the need for manufacturing, placing, and servicing of these mediums will continue. (We're not ignoring cable TV, and will discuss that in the next chapter.)

Most likely you have twisted pair copper wiring connecting your home phone system to a local phone system, or "local loop." Believe it or not, a ribbon of copper telephone wire stretching over 1 billion miles already blankets local loops from coast to coast. Unfortunately, this local loop is too limited to transmit high speed multimedia data, video, and voice without causing the equivalent of a transmission traffic jam.

What about fiber-optic cable? It happens to be an excellent medium for high speed, broadband transmission. Virtually all phone calls other than the local loop now use fiber-optic or are in the process of going to fiber-optic. This medium is also utilized within corporate and university networks to send high speed video and data.

The question is this: Is there a technology that gets the most out of both mediums, especially all those millions of miles of existing twisted pair copper wire?

That hope may rest with technologies like ISDN (Integrated Services Digital Network). ISDN makes it possible to simultaneously transmit all kinds of signals, from data to multimedia, over the network on both existing copper wires and fiber optic cables. This means, for example, that you can have *both* a phone call and a data transmission, or two phone calls going on at the same time through that one wire. Pretty nifty stuff. ISDN is already available in 80% of the United States. As it catches on, manufacturers of ISDN specified equipment and services will find opportunity.

While most ISDN equipment is located at the phone company, there will be a need for some basic home equipment to connect your home to the ISDN network and to convert the signal from your existing phone into a digital one that ISDN can understand.

Manufacturers like Motorola **(205-430-8000)** put these two functions into one box, so you'll just plug in and away you go!

ISDN will also generate new opportunities for those designing and manufacturing telephones. That's because ISDN will let you plug your phone into your computer. And not just any phone, but a new breed of smart telephone providing such conveniences as voice mail and a digital display for both lines.

Case Study–

Remember, that just like the industrial revolution, the digital revolution needs engines to make it run. The infrastructure of the new high speed networks, whether wired or wireless, will require a whole new set of advanced switches, receivers, and transmitters.

Tekelec **(818-880-5656)**, a company headquartered in Calabasas, California, is one of those companies designing and manufacturing the testing devices and switching systems necessary to upgrade the telecommunications infrastructure of tomorrow.

In turn, there has been an upsurge in specialized components like laser diodes and high-performance semiconductors.

√√ *Wireless Communications*

If you decide to get into the wireless technologies area, either as an engineer or in sales and marketing, you'll need to understand the advantages that mobile networking has to offer. You'll also need to understand the different approaches to sending data and voice over the air.

Suffice it to say that wireless technologies include satellite links, radio, infrared transmission, cellular, microwave, and personal communications services (also known as micro-cellular).

The important thing to note here is that each transmission method is widely accepted, and that companies are utilizing these wireless technologies in different ways to improve service and productivity.

Case Study–

The growth of wireless devices is evidenced in their effective use by field reps, who instantly transmit the data to their company's home office computer. The UPS driver who picks up or delivers your packages, as well as other fleet service and dispatch companies, use two-way paging and wireless transmissions to keep track of your precious cargo's status, right up-to-the-minute.

Motorola **(205-430-8000)** has long been a leader in pagers and wireless data networks that let field reps send in orders and other data while on the road. IBM manufactures a wireless radio modem card that fits into laptop computers. Once the cost of transmission and hardware becomes more competitive, wireless communications will fly.

☞ NEW OPPORTUNITY

Personal Communications Services

Personal communications services, or PCS, is a new area of wireless communications. The

PCS frequencies that were put up by auction in 1993 will eventually be developed into hundreds of applications.

Handheld devices can be specialized to give up-to-the-minute information about traffic accidents, restaurant menus and prices, weather reports, movies, stocks, and travel services. And since PCS is an all-digital technology, the signal will be able to carry more information than analog systems.

PCS requires a major investment in the manufacture and installation of thousands of localized radio transceivers and other equipment. The result: PCS will be a boon to engineers, manufacturers, and installers who migrate from the defense industry into new communications fields.

One company, Qualcomm Incorporated (619-587-1121), has developed a new technology to link together existing telephone services with PCS. Major telecommunications companies like Sprint (404-859-5000) and TCI (303-267-5500) have agreed to use Qualcomm's technology. As an example of how the emerging wireless network means untold jobs and opportunities in the near future, Qualcomm almost tripled its number of employees between 1994 and 1995.

CHAPTER 4

ON-LINE & COMMUNICATIONS SERVICES

"The new electronic interdependence recreates the world in the image of a global village."
Marshall McLuhan

Industry Snapshot

Welcome to a thriving frontier outpost. It's the one with the *juice*, an electrifying place where the air is pregnant with expectation and the dreams of Bill Gates wanna bees. They're all searching for the frontier's holy grail: Interactivity.

If you're looking for dealmakers, stockbrokers,

agents, enthusiastic entrepreneurs, venture capitalists, and prime cyber estate, then you've come to the right place. Of course, be prepared to meet a few hundred (hundred thousand?) cyber lawyers as well.

You'll have ample opportunity to meet with the denizens of this outpost at the much frequented Talk Is Cheap Saloon. (While you're there, keep a watchful eye on your wallet or purse.)

The nice thing about this outpost is that you don't have to have much money to stake a claim. Of course, the value of that claim is another matter. Hopefully, the sectors you visit at this outpost will spark a few ideas and opportunities.

On-line Gold Rush of the '90s

According to Simba Information, Inc., consumer on-line services ballooned to 11.8 million subscribers, reflecting a 26% increase in the second quarter of 1995.

No wonder that America Online **(703-448-8700)**, Prodigy **(800-PRODIGY)**, and CompuServe **(800-848-8199)** are like the ABC, CBS, and NBC of the on-line world.

These big three computer networks pioneered interactivity, making it easy to access a broad range of services and products, including the Internet. With over 11 million subscribers between them, their potential for growth is huge. There's also the popularity of the Internet, which offers its own world of interactivity.

There's an on-line gold rush in the works, with people staking claim to new territories and technologies in the hope of striking it rich. Some do. Usually, it's whoever provides an interactive, purposeful, and immediate connection with the on-line community.

The Opportunities are in the Interactivity

It comes down to this– if you are looking for jobs and opportunities in this sector, seek out those areas where there's a high degree of interactivity. To really comprehend this sector, explore as many of these areas as you can, not just in this book, but by joining the on-line community.

Interactivity is a powerful tool. Why? It's because on-line interactivity and usage are measurable. This is tantamount to having every user be a Nielson family that instantly registers what it likes and will spend money on. Basically, it's an advertiser's penultimate dream.

To get a piece of the interactive pie, major communications companies are either acquiring or forming strategic alliances with others who possess the digital tools of the future. This corporate move towards vertical integration is combining entertainment and telecommunications entities.

OCCUPATIONAL OPPORTUNITIES FOR:

- **Computer Programmers**

- **Data Communications Analysts**

- **Educators**

- **Entrepreneurs**

- **Graphic Designers**

- **Industrial Designers**

- **Interactive Television Directors**

- **Journalists**

- **Marketing Staff**

- **MIS & Network Administrators**

- **Multimedia Producers**

- **Product Design and Management**

- **Publishers**

- **Software Engineers**

- **Systems Analysts and Engineers**

- **Systems Operators**

- **Multimedia Designers**

- **Writers and Instructional Designers**

Interactive TV

It's more likely that Tele-Communications Inc. chairman John Malone will be remembered for introducing the idea of "500 channels" than for anything else he might do. That is, if he really makes that 500 channel prediction come true. Besides, you're probably thinking "who can watch that much TV? Aren't there already 500 daytime talk show hosts?" And you'd probably be right. Still, the promise of video-on-demand (VOD) and interactive TV (ITV) are helping thrust the technology towards this conclusion. This is, after all, the holy grail of the digital frontier!

> *"Television is an invention that permits you to be entertained in your living room by people you wouldn't have in your home."* David Frost

David Frost might have been correct back in 1971. But now, thanks to interactive TV, information and home shopping junkies can invite into their homes exactly what they want: Specialized news programs, customized shopping, and on-line game shows where they would be a virtual audience or even better, one of the contestants.

The glitch may be the cost of providing this level of interactive technology. It could cost cable and phone companies billions of dollars to rewire a new broadband network, or to bring together the patchwork of different networks that are already out there. And, there's the cost for the home set-top box that would provide for interactivity.

On-line and traditional media are transforming themselves daily. The opportunities here will multiply as our expectations and dependence on interactivity grow with each passing day.

√√ *Where to do it, Cable or Phone?*

Those working in technical, installation, network, manufacturing, service, communications, and creative fields all stand to benefit from the effort to converge technologies, services, and entertainment into a form of interactive television. Of course, no one is 100% certain how this interactivity is going to work or how much it will cost. Cable companies and phone companies are looking for the technologies that will let them provide interactive TV.

There is already a frantic rush to build the infrastructure for the interactive networks, set-top boxes, and create interesting content for those program hungry 500 channels.

Case Study–

Cable companies are pinning their hopes of interactivity on adding fiber-optic cable to the coaxial cable. Fiber-optic cable allows for either more channels or for some two-way interactivity.

Major cable systems like Time Warner **(212-484-8000)** and Tele-Communications Inc. **(303-267-5500)** have already upgraded a large percentage of their systems. Many are simply using the extra channels to deliver movies more frequently, such as every 15 minutes. This is known as "near-video-on-demand," and it begs the question of when do we get the real thing?

In an effort to deliver true interactivity, cable companies are looking to a hybrid fiber-coaxial cable that offers significantly higher capacity. Time Warner and others are experimenting with providing several channels of compressed video and interactivity over a single hybrid fiber-coaxial cable.

There is also AT&T's development of a higher capacity broadband network that will bring fiber-optic cable close to the home. This system has the potential of achieving the vaunted 500 channel capacity, plus interactivity.

According to a survey, the following graphs indicate the four highest and four lowest areas of consumer interest in interactivity.

What are Our Interactive Interests?

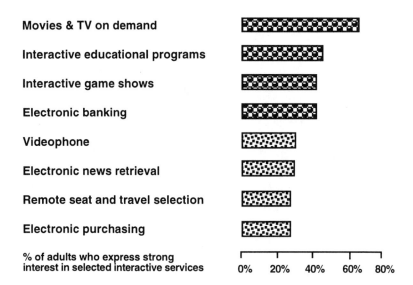

Movies & TV on demand	
Interactive educational programs	
Interactive game shows	
Electronic banking	
Videophone	
Electronic news retrieval	
Remote seat and travel selection	
Electronic purchasing	

% of adults who express strong
interest in selected interactive services

0%   20%   40%   60%   80%

Source: 1994 American Information User Survey, Find/SVP

Internet & World Wide Web

Many people equate the Internet with the digital frontier. Actually, it's only a sector of the frontier. What makes it special is that it's growing by leaps and bounds and is garnering interest from all corners of the world. And so, you may be asking: What exactly is the Internet? Why the excitement? And most importantly, what are the jobs and opportunities in this sector? Let's take these questions one at a time.

99

A Really, Really Big Show

The Internet is a massive international computer network– one that is made up of other computer networks. Basically, all of the computers within the Internet(work) support a standard protocol that allow them to communicate with each other. (Okay, so it's not really *that* simple.) So what you've got are all these global networks combined into the "Mother of All Computer Networks"!

The opportunity which seems to have blossomed overnight goes to those who learn those skills needed to become Internet developers. These developers will design and build Internet Web sites. Already, schools are offering training classes specializing in Internet developer certification (See Resource 2 & Resource 4).

The excitement about the Internet stems from the fact that it allows, even encourages, a democratic exchange of information, discourse, and other communications among millions of Internet users. More specifically, much of the Internet is used for E-mail, for gathering and distributing information, and for participating in on-line newsgroups (there are over 18,000 newsgroups). For years, the military and academic community used the Internet to disseminate information, articles, and papers.

It is estimated that the number of people on the Internet will multiply to over *500 million* by year 2000. As the Internet becomes popularized, its digital capabilities are being prevailed upon to build new markets for a range of products and services. In turn, business opportunities are germinating and evolving at a rapid rate. There's also the World Wide Web, aka WWW or the Web, which is a means of gaining access to the Internet that lets you randomly link from one Internet server (host computer) to another.

The Internet is so vast that it's difficult to keep up

with what exists on it. The following sections will give you a better idea of how the Internet and Web are being used and how those uses translate into jobs and opportunities. Consider getting an Internet directory, such as Osborne McGraw-Hill's *The Internet Yellow Pages*, or IDG Books' *Yahoo Unplugged: Your Discovery Guide to the Net*, as useful tools for navigating and understanding the Internet's offerings.

By reading all the sections below, you'll get a grasp of not just opportunities and jobs, but a sense of the Internet and its great potential. If you're specifically interested in knowing how to use the Internet to search for jobs, you'll want to check out Resource 1 of this book.

☞ NEW OPPORTUNITY

> ### Internet Access Provider
> ### &
> ### Web Farmer

You've got a computer, a telephone, and a modem. And you've read about the Internet and decide you'd like to connect to it. So all you need is the phone number, right? Wrong! Let's put it this way– unless you know the Unix computer language and your computer supports something called the TCP/IP protocol you'd have a lot better luck speaking English to a Frenchman.

The need for non-technical people to connect to the Internet has created a demand for people who make the Internet's technology accessible to the average user. Consider that in the Los Angeles area alone, there are over 50 major Internet access providers– national and local– all competing for your business.

Internet access providers make it possible for your computer's Window, Mac, Unix, OS/2, or other interface to have the connection and software it needs to link up with and speak Internet's language. As a result, you'll be able to use some of the Internet's new graphical tools and services (such as World Wide Web, as mentioned below).

Or maybe you would like to be a Web Farmer? Here's how. Some providers do more than simply offer software and a connection to the Internet. As a full service provider you could offer total maintenance of a customer's Internet server and Web site. In essence, you'd be cultivating and caring for hundreds of computers in a maze of racks and wires, all blaring out information and linking up to other computers around the globe!

Someone will no doubt seize this opportunity to become the architect of a McDonalds-style Web Farm franchise. Then, as you sign on, you'll see a brief message that brags, "Over a hundred billion connections served."

If you're looking to get into the provider and Web farming business, you'll need a staff of experts fluent in Unix, networking, and the Internet, plus lots of technical support to keep customers happy. Don't forget those sales reps!

☞ NEW JOB AREA

Web Page Designer

This should be of special interest to graphic artists, graphic designers, writers with a knowledge of graphics tools, computer layout artists, industrial designers, and animators.

Whereas the Internet provides boring-looking screens that are full of text, the World Wide Web allows graphics and a user-friendly environment via Web pages.

You'll search for signs of intelligence on the Web by using software products called Web browsers (usually provided by your Internet Access Provider). Then, in a matter of moments, you'll be linked up with the appropriate Web site and Web pages.

A Web home page is the first one a visitor sees. It needs to convey a sense of all the content at that site. Many Web pages contain interactive buttons that you can click on, and which link you to other pages. Just think of these pages as billboards for whoever has that page. There's been a big move for companies, consultants, retailers, publishers, and others to get a presence on the Internet by creating their own World Wide Web pages.

Just like a good billboard, each Web page has to be well designed to get attention. Web pages can combine text, graphics, and even virtual reality environments. They'll also need to be formatted in the Web's HTML language, as well as be linked to other pages.

Web page designers need to become proficient at using Web linking tools and computer graphics programs. Keep in mind that some Internet Access Providers also offer Web page setups with their service. Do you need to know HTML in order to design Web pages? Read on for the answer.

√√ *Web Software*

There is excellent news ahead for Web software engineers and developers. Web software sales are exploding, and they are expected to multiply more than tenfold from 1995 to 1996. That equates to an increase in sales from $260 million to about $4 billion.

Software applications of all kinds are needed to service the Web. These include authoring programs for Web pages, tools for setting up Web sites and servers, audio and graphics tools for building a multimedia Web environment, tools for marketing and tracking Web usage, as well as search and retrieval programs to scan the Internet for information.

Products for mass consumption will be personal Web publishing programs that help average Web users who lack programming skills to set up their own Web pages and sites. The latest layout programs, such as PageMaker, include built-in Web authoring tools to format and link text. The good news for non-computer techies is that such features obviate the need for learning the Web's HTML language. Even word processors are incorporating easy-to-use Web tools.

These new tools will be ideal for organizing a

collection of information into one Web page or several pages. Web designers create more than just single pages of information. Usually, they build multiple pages that are linked together by topics, words, or hot spots that users can click on. These pages create a total environment for obtaining information on a particular subject, company, product, or service.

Case Study–

While some software developers are redesigning their programs to incorporate Web tools, others like Netscape Communications Corporation, are seizing the opportunity to create a whole new class of software products tailored to make the Web easier and faster to use.

Mountain View, California-based Netscape **(415-528-2555 & http://home.netscape.com)** offers the full-featured Netscape Navigator browser for searching the Web, along with a host of other Web related tools.

In addition to Web browsers, dedicated Web authoring software will bring on-line publishing within reach of the non-technical on-line user. Users will be able to create Web documents, edit them, and place them on-line.

With these tools, you'll be creating graphical and multimedia environments with a click of the mouse. In essence, this bold capability will do as much to transform on-line communications into a powerful medium as word processing did to transform publishing.

☞ NEW OPPORTUNITY

On-line Publishing

Have you ever wished you could buy a book and have an electronic version of it downloaded into your personal computer within minutes? It's already happening, and here's why it makes sense: Each year, over 50,000 new books are published. This means that for each year's batch of new books to make it into the stores, most of the existing books would have to be tossed off the shelf! Many books simply don't get the wide distribution they need to reach their audience. The cost of marketing, printing, and shipping books adds up.

For very small or alternative publications, there's now the option of publishing on the Internet. The advantages? First of all, there's no cost for paper or printing. And, you have the choice to publish short pieces using Web pages, or to offer downloads of the electronic file versions of your work. (For creating interactive books, see Chapter 2's section on Electronic Publishing.)

BiblioBytes is an Internet publisher that specializes in electronic books. With over 500 electronic books available, BiblioBytes entices writers and book publishers with the promise of increased sales. Downloadable books come in many formats (ASCII, RTF, etc.) and are offered over the Internet.

106

TRENDS 2000:

Hypertextbooks

You're having trouble grasping some of the concepts in that darn chemistry or math class you're taking. Fortunately, your textbook is hyperlinked to the Internet. This means you may utilize resources like expert interviews, interactive exercises, microscopic images, and a handy glossary of terms.

Already, colleges and high schools are experimenting with hypertextbooks. Over 20 universities and high schools are participating in Calculus and Mathematica, *an on-line course. The course lets students work on equations and plot results in real-time. And yes, homework assignments are given on-line, too!*

Other hypertextbook experiments include one being pioneered at the University of Iowa. The subject?: Shakespeare's Henry V. *If reading Shakespeare leaves you cold, the hypertextbook version will help enliven the process with famous film clips, definitions of antiquated Elizabethan terms, and background information.*

This is bound to be a booming area for educators, writers, publishers, artists, and others who will help to shape and create the first generation of hypertextbooks.

☞ NEW OPPORTUNITY

On-line Catalogs

The creation of interactive catalogs makes for a great opportunity for creative and business people to be at the forefront of the Internet revolution by creating new kinds of content and connections. Since the Internet is crammed with information, the trick is to package that information in ways that make it easy to access and useful for users.

The realm of music, which consists of thousands of musical selections and bands, is a perfect example. Several Web sites provide and organize music for Internet users. The Internet Underground Music Archive *lists upcoming, independent bands whose musical selections are easily downloaded for sampling. Bringing music directly into the home (okay, computer) is a powerful use of the medium. Other music sites offer catalogs of recording companies, music stores, and even bands themselves.*

The ability to send music over the Internet is making music cataloging a hot area. Many of these Web sites possess all the pizzazz of MTV, and are often designed by a mix of graphic designers, writers, programmers, directors, and musicians.

There are many other excellent uses for this "searchable" medium. Retailers, universities, and even museums are using the Internet and World Wide Web to provide catalogs promoting their services and products.

√√ *Business-Oriented Databases*

While consumer on-line services and the Web are great tools for entertainment and marketing, there's also a need for industrial strength on-line information. For years, businesses, law firms, and investment companies have been using heavy duty databases.

If you build a solid database, they will come. And, they will pay handsomely for the information. The case study below illustrates how one company is using the World Wide Web to go beyond marketing and put useful content on-line.

Case Study–

The Thomas Register of American Manufacturers is available on-line through Dialog and CompuServe. In 1995, however, Thomas Publishing Company **(212-290-7291 & http://www.thomasregister.com)** also built a dedicated Web site for its vast Thomas Register database.

The Thomas Register Web database contains over 50,000 service and product categories, under which it lists more than 190,000 companies. Through the Web, users can directly access the database to easily locate sources for almost any product.

Keep in mind that Thomas Publishing Company didn't design, build, and maintain its Web site. Instead, the firm hired expert consultants. But if you have the right information, cataloging or database software, and the right programming tools for the Web, then you could create your own industrial strength site or do it for someone else.

☞ NEW JOB AREA

Cyber Researcher

You know how to surf the net for the most arcane information in a moment's time. You are wired in to Dow Jones News/Retrieval **(609-520-4000)***, Lexis/Nexis* **(800-227-4908)***, NewsNet* **(800-345-1301)***, and Dialog* **(800-334-2564)***. To top it off, you've memorized Dialog's vast business-oriented system of over 500 separate databases.*

You also know exactly where to go to dig out the latest information on merger rumors, stock splits, and financials. You know which magazines and journals are on which service and how to search them quickly. You know what listserv has the experts you were hired to query.

To the average Joe, you are a computer dweeb. But to your boss, or to the executive, publisher, or CEO who hires you, you are a cyber researching genius. And you're a well paid one who possesses an extremely valuable skill– especially since most people don't have the time or know-how to search the net.

You make a point of advertising your skills on your Web home page. Before you know it, word gets out and you soon have more business than you can handle.

110

☞ **NEW JOB AREA**

Cyber Journalist & Title Builder

You'd like to write a story without the usual constraints of newsprint space. You wish your readers could read the full text of the interview you conducted with the mayor. Better yet, how about including some sound bytes and a video clip of that interview? And finally, how about including all your notes, research documents, sources, and more with the article?

You can do all of the above as a cyber journalist because what was impossible to do with print journalism is reality in cyber space.

Layoffs continue to plague the ranks of experienced newspaper and magazine journalists. Fortunately, new media is taking up the slack.

*On-line Web services such as Politics USA (**http://www.politicsusa.com**) and CNN (**http://www.cnn.com**) are creating cyber newsrooms. Politics USA, for example, is a niche Web publication dedicated to covering presidential campaign politics. Expect a proliferation of niche on-line publications to keep journalists busy. (Remember Nanothinc from Chapter 4?)*

New on-line services like Microsoft Network

and Delphi are giving cyber journalists a chance to explore stories in greater depth than was previously possible. Eventually, photographs, graphics, hyperlinks, and even video and sound bytes will be the usual elements of any story.

Microsoft Network also employs "Title Builders." While they may not be full-fledged journalists, Title Builders are people with some news experience whose job it is to hyperlink headline titles and keywords so that the electronic news service is an interactive, searchable database.

Videoconferencing

Videoconferencing is probably one of the more misunderstood sectors of the digital frontier. Real world use of two-way video for executive conferences has expanded to include hiring, sales, and product demonstrations. The primary benefit: Substantial savings from the cost of travel. In truth, the technology goes far beyond simply connecting groups of persons in different locations.

Jobs and opportunities will go to those who can build and design cost effective software and hardware videoconferencing tools, as well as network and MIS staff who manage the systems.

The ability to send not only video, but to share data and information between desktop computers is causing a considerable migration to desktop videoconferencing. This trend is revolutionizing the corporate culture and workplace, and is responsible for the industry more than doubling its revenue from over $30 million in 1994 to $80 million in 1995.

√√ *Long Distance Learning*

Knowing how to capitalize on the realm of long distance learning presents new challenges for writers, as well as curriculum and instructional designers. Generally, long distance learning courses must be designed to include interactivity, and some courses require a minimum of 15 minutes of interactivity for every 50 minutes of classroom time. Coursework and textbooks, for example, need to be rewritten and organized to fit this new learning paradigm.

Already, there's an Electronic University Network **(800-225-3276)** that includes associate, bachelors, and masters programs. Courses combine videotape, text, software, and on-line interactive classes that bring together instructors and students. The Electronic University is accessed through America Online and includes technical support, use of library facilities, and other AOL services.

Depending on the complexity, long distance learning sites may require specialized network equipment, such as satellite dishes, videos camera at each site, and computers to run the videoconferencing software that manages the whole process. Those with video, instructional, and computer technical expertise will find many opportunities in this area.

Over 75% of the workforce will need retraining by year 2000, states the American Society for Training and Development. If so, then the classroom of the future might resemble the novel approach to communicating and learning provided by long distance learning.

Have you ever taken a self-paced study course or used an instructional video? All the information is directed towards you, the viewer. Two important elements make long distance learning vastly different from other learn at home programs. First, as the name implies, students needn't be in the same location as the teacher. Second, there's a high level of interactivity because both sides can respond, interrupt, and interact as if they were in a real classroom.

How do long distance learning networks work? Well, they can be either relatively simple or very complex. Some use basic telephone service, others employ ISDN (discussed in Chapter 3, Wired Communications), and still others broadcast over private wireless satellite networks. However, not all videoconferences are created equal. Image quality and interactivity is directly proportional to the cost.

Case Study–

In Alaska, there are schools where students watch and listen to their teacher just like in any classroom across the United States. The difference is that their teacher may be hundreds of miles away, lecturing to them via two-way, interactive video. A video camera in the classroom makes it possible for the teacher to see and hear the students, learn their names and faces, and even respond to their questions.

In Santa Monica, California, a local Chapter of the International Interactive Communications Society **(503-579-4427)** holds a two-way video meeting between its local members and a San Francisco-based software firm specializing in the design of virtual reality sets for the broadcasting industry. After a demonstration, both sides engage in a lively question and answer session.

In Bloomfield, Michigan, video and multimedia production company Visual Services, Inc. **(810-644-0500)** utilizes a private satellite network to beam interactive training programs to hundreds of Ford dealerships across the country. Sales and service staff taking the classes can communicate with other participants and the instructor via voice transmission. Students even take pop quizzes and tests by using a keypad that stores their responses in a computer.

TRENDS 2000:

Telecenters

You're the manager of a corporate division with headquarters in Los Angeles. But you live off the beaten path over 60 miles away in lush Laguna Beach. The morning drive to the office should take you an hour and a half, on a good day. But you arrive in just twenty minutes. How?

You do it by driving to one of Southern California's 20 telecenters. Once there, you've got a digital arsenal of computers, voice mail, high speed data lines, video-conferencing, and more, at your disposal.

California Telecenters service 100,000 of the region's total of over 600,000 telecommuters— almost 10% of the total workforce. Nationwide, it's estimated that over 8 million people telecommute.

The winning idea behind telecommuting is that is does more than save time, energy consumption, and stress. Telecommuting encourages new management techniques, and places a value on managing by objective and shared responsibility.

What are the services the new breed of telecommuters will need? Certainly, more accessible and useful telecenters are needed. Writers of "how-to succeed at telemanaging" books and training materials for telemanagers and telesupervisors will be in demand. And, telecenters will need to be marketed, managed, and staffed.

In Los Angeles and surrounding counties, several phone companies have joined with local governments to form the Southern California Telecommuting Partnership (800-6INFOHWY) for the express purpose of promoting telecommuting. Money raised by the group is used to establish and run its telecenters.

☞ NEW JOB AREA

Videoconferencing Director

Advanced long distance learning programs combine interactive video, graphics, video clips, and computer desktop images. To accomplish this seamlessly requires someone who is technically adept at both computer and video technology.

To help the process run smoothly, graphics charts, images, and video clips are often burned onto a CD-ROM laser disk. The technical director follows along with the instructor's manual and triggers the playing of other media at the proper time. It is also the responsibility of the videoconferencing director to let the instructor know if he or she is running over time.

Just like television shows, long distance learning classes are usually rehearsed and simulated before a course is broadcast.

CHAPTER 5

CREATIVE SERVICES

"The mind is an astonishing instrument; there is no man-made machinery that is so complex, subtle, with such infinite possibilities." *J. Krishnamurti*

Industry Snapshot

Welcome to the frontier's most glamorous outpost. Here, entertainment takes many forms, ranging from the latest video games to interactive music. The opportunities for creative types are boundless, with more jobs being forged all the time.

President Clinton's 1995 pledge to hook up schools to the Internet will only fuel the need for more and better content. As you travel this outpost, stop by the Content Is King Cafe, and you'll discover that high quality content truly is the key to this kingdom.

What's Popular at Home?

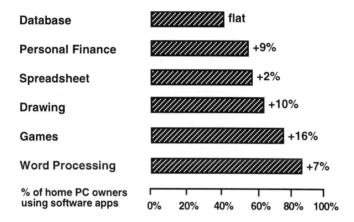

(Numbers next to bars indicate % change in share of households using this application since 1993)

Source: Direct Magazine, 1995

There's No Business Like Show Business

As content is created, so are more jobs and opportunities. Fortunately, the trend towards new media entertainment is opening the door for more fresh talent. Many existing companies are starting up interactive or new media divisions, such as Time Warner Electronic Publishing **(212-522-4643)**, Simon & Schuster Interactive **(212-698-7172)**, and Random House New Media **(212-751-2600)**, to name a few. But possessing a new media division doesn't guarantee success. The secret to understanding interactivity is in knowing how to use content in the new medium.

The same kind of creative people who make the entertainment world tick will drive new media. This includes computer savvy people like programmers and software engineers. If you're interested in becoming a star in one of the following fields, then have fun and check out this very creative outpost on the frontier.

OCCUPATIONAL OPPORTUNITIES FOR:

- **Actors**

- **Agents**

- **Animators**

- **Artists**

- **Computer Programmers**

- **Educators**

- **Entrepreneurs**

- **Film/Video Producers**

- **Game Designers**

- **Graphic Designers**

- **Instructional Designers**

- **Interactive Designers**

- **Lawyers**

- **Marketing Staff**

- **Musicians**

- **Product Designers and Managers**

- **Systems Engineers and Analysts**

- **Photographers**

- **Publishers**

- **Writers**

Edutainment

Simba Information Inc. reports that publisher revenue for educational multimedia CD-ROMs was expected to grow from $85 million in 1994 to $135 million in 1995. That's a growth of over 58%. As more and more families own PCs, the thirst for edutainment will increase. If you're looking to create this content, you'll need the answers to a few pertinent questions.

Learning at Any Age

For what age groups is edutainment being created? California-based *Club Kidsoft* (**800-354-6150**) is a software shopping club designed for kids ages 4 through 12. There's a quarterly magazine for members, plus some CD-ROM demos. The bottom line is that there's edutainment designed for preschoolers, elementary, high school, college, and adults, with fascinating explorations of topics ranging from the human body to exotic, distant lands.

☞ NEW JOB AREA

CD-ROM & Software Reviewer

Writers will appreciate this opportunity, which is made possible by hundreds of new CD-ROMs and software products.

*Creating the new educational, game, and entertainment software are a number of well known firms such as Microsoft **(206-882-8080)**, Disney Interactive **(818-543-4300)**, Edmark Corporation **(206-556-8484)**, and Sierra On Line Inc. **(209-683-4468)**, as well as some smaller companies like Knowledge Adventure **(818-542-4200)** and Elroy's Headbone Interactive **(206-323-0073)**.*

In addition, America Online, CompuServe, and Prodigy offer extensive shareware libraries containing a variety of educational and game software. With so much out there, it's impossible to know which CD-ROMS and software to buy. That's why we need to depend on knowledgeable reviewers to help us pick the winners and avoid the dogs. Who knows?– maybe you'll become the digital frontier's Siskel or Ebert!

You might want to check out guides such as Mike Langberg's CD-ROM Superguide, *Eric Brown's* That's Edutainment, *and the* Children's Software Revue *newsletter **(313-480-0040)**. There's also* PC Shareware **(800-447-2181)** *for a comprehensive catalog listing* *thousands of games for children. Even Newsweek has joined the reviewing bandwagon with its annual* CD-ROM, Parent's Guide to Children's Software.

If you don't want to create your own guide, consider reviewing CD-ROMS for magazines. Since there are CD-ROMS for most niche areas, find those magazines which match.

√√ *Learning and Edutainment Web Sites*

Educators and others looking to create content might want to explore *The Educator's Guide to the Internet*. This useful guide, published by the Virginia Space Grant Consortium, gives readers insight into the Internet's educational services. It also shows how to incorporate those many resources into lesson plans.

To get a better idea of what's out there, you can use the government as a good source of edutainment software. Best of all, it's provided for free. The U.S. Department of Education has a toll-free number **(800-222-4922)** to connect to your modem for downloading K-12 grade software directly into your computer.

For general learning, America Online offers students help with their homework by having volunteer teachers manning the network. Better yet, on-line services provide access to the World Wide Web. And it is through the emergence of the Web and hypertextbooks (Chapter 4) that Web sites will increasingly serve as a wellspring of edutainment.

Case Study–

Latitude 28 Schoolhouse is a global education Web site **(http:/www.packet.net/schoolhouse/)** that links up students with other schools, museums, and educational software libraries, games, digital coloring books, and more. The emphasis is on interactivity, and many of the most recent Web tools (extra programs that enhance the interactive experience) are included.

Students and teachers can search Latitude 28 Schoolhouse through a number of curriculum choices, including social studies, math, and science. The links are what make this site special, as it offers something for all ages and tastes. The social studies link, for example, connects to various government sites that encourage thought and participation in the democratic process.

Kids Web **(http:/www.infomall.org/kidsweb/)** is like a digital library of art, drama, and literature. In addition to a wide selection of on-line children's classics, fiction, and poetry, there's a Web art museum that's based on Paris' famous Louvre gallery.

Both Latitude 28 Schoolhouse and Kids Web are interested in linking with new educational sites. So contact them when you're up and running.

Electronic Property Rights

Multimedia, as an amalgam of text, images, video, and music, just may be the copyright lawyer's ultimate dream. Knowledge of electronic property rights for CD-ROMs and the on-line environment is definitely needed in this frontier outpost.

Law firms assign highly specialized technology groups to handle a whole spectrum of new media legal issues. These new media attorneys consult and advise businesses on issues involving software protection, information technologies, technology licensing and protection, intellectual property, multimedia, and corporate partnering that is technology based.

☞ NEW JOB AREA

Electronic Rights Specialist

Anyone contemplating, yet alone using multimedia must contend with the issue of electronic rights. And while there is no specific mention of electronic rights in the U.S. Copyright Act, electronic rights are included in copyright law.

Electronic rights include more than just content and can be complicated by referring to a work's style of format, distribution, reproduction, adaptation, and means of display. In short, there's a real need for lawyers who understand the subtleties of the electronic world.

One development that may help clarify electronic rights is a collaboration between the Corporation for National Research Initiatives (CNRI) and the Library of Congress. One day, electronic copyright registration and depositing of works will be possible. Eventually, this will result in an electronic rights database management system that will let multimedia producers license works via an extensive on-line network brimming with content.

Two books, Kirsch's Handbook of Publishing Law *by Johnathon Kirsch and* NetLaw: Your Rights in the Online World *by Lance Rose, provide the fundamentals for those lawyers*

126

interested in helping multimedia developers avoid property rights pitfalls.

LAWYER'S LEGAL RESOURCES

- **Copyright Office**
  (202) 707-3000

- **U.S. Patent and Trademark Office**
  (703) 308-HELP

- **American Intellectual Property Law Association**
  (703) 415-0780

- **Interactive Multimedia Association**
  (410) 626-1380

- **Software Patent Institute**
  (313) 769-4606

- **Software Publishers Association**
  (202) 452-1600

☞ **NEW OPPORTUNITY**

Multimedia Rights Clearance Agency and On-line Agent

The licensing of electronic property rights takes time. Too much time in some cases, since a multimedia CD-ROM can easily contain hundreds or thousands of copyrighted materials! Rather than search them all one at a time, there has to be an easier way.

Some developers hire rights clearance agencies which track down the owner of the rights and then negotiate the contracts. Already, there are companies specializing in music, video, and photos.

As the multimedia market matures, there will surely be a need for on-line agents to handle electronic rights for specialized material. Consider that pictorial, fine art, and graphic art are copyrightable and will one day be used in CD-ROMs. Those artists and sculptors whose work can be "touched" from within virtual reality art galleries (Chapter 7), will need representation.

On-line agents, who may or may not be attorneys, won't supplant the existing music and stock photo libraries, but only serve to popularize new forms of art and music.

Entertainment & Multimedia

Traditional forms of entertainment are entering a new era. The tools needed to create multimedia entertainment are on the desktop and are no longer the exclusive domain of Hollywood powerbrokers. This is not to say that Hollywood won't be a player– they'll just be creating more sophisticated and spectacular cutting edge products than anyone else.

The multimedia industry has yet to hit its stride. It is

estimated that, at present, only a small percentage of multimedia titles attain profitability. This will inevitably change as distribution channels become more established and publishers hone their products to meet niche market demands.

When bookstores begin demonstrating CD-ROMs for customers, then they will begin selling in big numbers. In the meantime, publishers are producing titles as prolifically as ever.

One excellent reference that profiles over 80 multimedia publishers is *Multimedia '95: Beyond Games*. This special supplement is a collaboration of *Publishers Weekly* **(800-362-8433)**, *Library Journal*, and *School Library*. The publication focuses on publishers who develop a full range of products for children, as well as entertainment, edutainment, reference, and some games for adults.

What follows are a melange of digital applications for the entertainment and multimedia sectors. The skills you will need are as diverse as the jobs and opportunities that are described. Happy cyber hunting!

√√ *Digital Film Studio*

Hollywood is rapidly embracing digital processes, from the editing of films to the transmission of movie clips to sound designers over high speed networks. The goal? A synergistic culture where the production cycle is shortened and a group of digital professionals can work on the film with instant results.

Case Study–

Dreamworks SKG **(818-733-7000)** is working with IBM to create what Spielberg, Katzenberg, and Geffen envision as Hollywood's first all digital movie studio. To this end, IBM's Digital Library software is the cornerstone in helping store, manage, and deliver the digital elements necessary for producing animated and live action feature films, television programs, and CD-ROM multimedia titles.

Paramount Pictures used a networked bank of five nonlinear editing systems hooked up to 120 gigabytes of storage to work on the film *Virtuosity*. Sound, visual effects, graphics, and other digital media were imported to build an edited, digital version of the film.

The Open Media Framework Interchange System **(http://www.illustra.com/~omf/OMF_Home_Page. html)** is a new standard for digital media that helps to create a means for integrating digital applications.

As a trend of things to come, the University of Southern California in 1995 established its first-ever *Entertainment Technology Center* **(213-740-6207)**, dedicated to training tomorrow's multimedia experts. Many universities with Cinema and Television departments are following suit as a demand for digital skills creates a whole new degreed course of study.

☞ NEW JOB AREA

Interactive Designer

Multimedia entertainment requires a strong concept, a consistent visual look, interactive elements, graphics and animation, sound effects, music, and a dramatic sense of story. How all this is brought together is the job of the interactive designer. Such a person is part artist, part storyteller, part graphic designer, yet may not be the sole creator of any of these individual pieces.

The interactive designer uses a multimedia authoring program (Chapter 2) to bring all the multimedia elements into sync. From which disciplines do such designers come? Actually, they often have previous experience as artists, animators, computer layout designers, educators, and writers. At the very least, it's essential for an interactive designer to be proficient in computer graphics.

How do you land a job as an interactive designer? Generally, this area is so new that on-the-job training is not unusual. One sure way of getting into this field is to master multimedia authoring programs such as Digital Box Office *from PowerProduction Software* **(310-937-4411),** Director *from Macromedia* **(800-288-4797),** *and* Oracle Media Objects *from Oracle Corporation* **(415-506-7000).**

Better yet, create some of your own multimedia samples as a calling card when you contact multimedia developers.

☞ NEW JOB AREA

Interactive Writer

Good stories carry you away on an emotional journey. A good interactive story does the same thing, but in a new way. It must be designed to encourage participation by the user in the story process itself. To do this, the user is presented with a variety of choices or perspectives from which to view the story. The result should be an experience that is unique.

The CD-ROM MYST is a wonderful example of an involving, nonlinear story that is told through hundreds of branches, or paths, from which you choose. Each choice links you to a multitude of other branches. When done right, the effect is a very satisfying and cumulative building up of suspense, knowledge, and surprise. Multimedia writing templates (Chapter 2) will make branches and links easy for the writer to follow and to test out. There are also flow chart programs that can help a writer develop a branching story structure.

Firms like Los Angeles-based Philips Media (310-444-6600) use writers to develop their interactive multiplatform CD-ROMs. And don't forget to explore the business market. Corporations and government agencies, such as Apria Healthcare and California's Orange County Transit Authority, routinely use interactive kiosks and CD-ROMs to sell products, services, and train their employees.

TRENDS 2000:

Interactive Comics

Comic fans devour over 200 million comics and graphic novels yearly. Perhaps no other entertainment form better lends itself to the digital realm than do comics. Once fully developed, this new entertainment form may well surpass the old in popularity.

Digital comics will do what comics do best– create a powerful and engaging visual world. Only they will probably do it better, thanks to more dynamic textures, colors, graphics effects, 3-D environments, the addition of sound effects, music, some video and limited animation, and most important of all, interactivity.

Digital comics break out of the comic page and comic frame format. They'll resemble scenes from films, and interactivity will be used as a storytelling tool.

Digital, interactive comics are labor intensive, and comic artists of tomorrow will need to be versed in computer drawing and coloring. They'll need to learn 3-D and virtual reality imaging tools. The process may still have specialists, such as artists for drawing and designing backgrounds (although these may be in 3-D), character artists, and computer colorists.

The writers of the comic will work with interactive designers (this Chapter), who program all the elements with an authoring tool. In addition, production will include a staff of freelancers to provide video and music as needed.

> *How will users obtain digital comics?: On CD-ROM or as a daily comic strip available on the Web and on-line services.*
>
> *To that end, firms like Los Angeles-based ZMedia Inc. and New York-based Byron Preiss Multimedia publish daily interactive comic strips for the on-line environment.*

√√ *Multimedia Mapping*

There are many unique ways of combining visuals, graphics, and sound. Advances in the digital frontier are causing as great a revolution for map makers as advances in electronic publishing are causing for publishers.

At the core of digital mapping is something called Geographic Information Systems, or GIS. Like multimedia, GIS combines computer aided design graphics, database information, digitized maps, animation, video, voice, and even background music. Of course, Geographic Information Systems can be used to create some fascinating multimedia travel guides, as well as multidimensional navigational maps.

Case Study–

Onboard automobile navigation systems are one use of digital mapping which is already active in certain cities. While these maps are two-dimensional, they are still impressive in their ability to track a vehicle's location using a signal from a satellite.

Other, somewhat more accessible and popular uses of multimedia mapping are being plumbed by Atlas publishers. One CD-ROM, *Street Atlas USA*, published by DeLorme Mapping **(800-452-5931)**, has ranked among the top ten highest rated personal productivity software products.

DeLorme's *Street Atlas USA* lets the user zoom in and out of areas of choice. Geographical zones can be selected by city name, zip code, and area code. In addition to getting more details when zooming in, you also get lists of major sites of interest, from zoos to museums. When you're done searching, you can print out sections as needed.

Freeport, Maine-based DeLorme Mapping also offers a *Global Explorer* CD-ROM that links map sections to a database of cultural, economic, and other useful information. As these products become more sophisticated, they could more accurately map geographical locations and weather systems as seen from outer space by incorporating both video and high resolution photo images.

Keep in mind that the backgrounds, imagery, characters, and screen layouts in games and other products keeps growing more advanced. That means that over time, the skills of multimedia developers, designers, artists, photographers, writers, and other creative people will be at a premium.

√√ *Computer Animation*

Computer animation has been around for quite awhile. So, what's new about it, you ask? For those in the know, it would be the buzz surrounding the first-ever fully computer animated feature film.

Just which studio would you expect to be attached to such a film? Need we say more than the name Disney? But what's different about the film *Toy Story* is that it was created by the feature production division of a computer software and animation company: Pixar Animation Studios.

Disney and Pixar are only the tip of the iceberg for

feature film animation. While Time-Warner develops its own feature animation division, Time-Warner Interactive **(818-295-6623)** is busily planning to release at least 10 new multimedia titles yearly.

Case Study–

The staff of over 100 people who were hired by Richmond, California-based Pixar Animation Studios **(510-236-4000)** to work on *Toy Story* had eclectic backgrounds. Their skills ranged from knowledge of architecture and theater, to backgrounds in claymation and traditional animation.

The amazing point of it all is that the film represents an entertainment form created from within the computer. Characters, sets, and objects consist of digital information, all of it modeled, rendered, and textured inside the computer. True, the movie features the very human voices of stars Tom Hanks and Tim Allen. But one day...

Games

The Software Publishing Association's 1994 survey found that CD-ROM sales jumped a whopping 229% over 1993 sales figures. Of the $647.5 million in sales, the category of games and other home entertainment software accounted for the largest share ($169.2 million) and represented a 275% increase from the previous year. These numbers don't even include the lucrative video game market.

Typically, the top selling software game products are distinctly unique from one another. Some of 1995's popular game products bear this out. There's the Star Wars style 3-D shooting game *Dark Forces* by LucasArts Entertainment **(800-782-7927)**, adventure mystery *Myst* by Brøderbund **(800-521-6263)**, shooting game *Doom II* by GT Interactive **(800-332-4300)**, and role playing game *Descent* by Interplay **(800-969-4263)**.

Because most games are extremely labor intensive to create, the games sector is a fast paced environment. The best game designers, programmers, and animation artists contend for big dollars.

For competitive companies, game programmers' salaries reach into the low six figure range; artists earn about half as much; executive game producers may be rewarded with earnings of up to $150,000 a year. But, be prepared to work grueling hours under constant pressure. What follows are some areas of interest for true "gamers."

☞ NEW JOB AREA

Game Tester

You frequently sit glassy-eyed for hours of nonstop playing with Donkey Kong and Super Mario Brothers. You know game lingo, have an ability to communicate, and are always finding "bugs" in the games you play. If this description fits you, then you probably have what it takes to be a game tester.

Testing is crucial to the development of any video or software game. Searching for computer bugs takes time, lots of it. But then you get paid for your efforts. Sega of America (800-872-7342) brings game testers together at its Redwood City, California-based testing center. Sega, creator of the Sega Genesis game player and Sonic the Hedgehog fame, employs over 100 video game testers to check the integrity of its games. When Christmas rolls around, the testing can go around the clock.

This job may also be of special interest to those who are looking to one day design and produce their own games.

If you want to know who to call for game testing, pick up an interactive entertainment magazine such as Electronic Entertainment (415-349-4300). Along with game reviews and lists of the top rated games are the contact numbers for game publishers.

☞ NEW OPPORTUNITY

Interactive Movies & Games

It's a game. No, it's a movie. No, it's a game. Actually, what's going on is the new trend towards making films that are also games. Shot on actual soundstages, interactive movies plunge you into the action more convincingly than does a visit to the local cineplex.

It was as recently as 1993 that Trilobyte's The 7th Guest *CD-ROM burst onto the scene as one of the first games to effectively use live action video. It sold 1.5 million copies. The company's follow-up interactive movie,* The 11th Hour, *took two years of work from computer programmers alone!*

Legitimate stars are now appearing on CD-ROMs for play on the desktop. Pamela Lee, star of the feature film Barb Wire, *is slated to appear in the Dark Horse Interactive (503-652-8815) computer game version of* Barb Wire. *While budgets for these full motion video games can be in the millions, they pale in comparison with the cost of the average feature film.*

Again, computer skills put you in the driver's seat. Designers of computer generated sets, images, and backgrounds that comprise much of these products' otherworldly sci-fi locales and ambiance will find high paying job security.

Likewise, those interactive designers and developers who understand the delicate balance between cinematic action and game playing will find themselves in demand.

√√ *Multiplayer Gaming Networks*

If the idea of role playing on your computer– being the Red Baron and fighting against someone thousands of miles away– fascinates you, then you can understand why Multiplayer Gaming, or MPG, is a sector of the frontier that's catching fire.

In recognition of the potential of these MPG environments, AT&T in 1994 purchased a nationwide game net, ImagiNation Network **(800-462-4461 & http://www.inngames.com)**. How do MPGs work?

Game players sign on to a game playing network

where they pay an hourly fee to join in on the fun. Even casino-style gambling networks have sprung up (how long such services will remain on-line, who knows?). To make MPG networks run requires the help of computer programmers, network engineers, animators, game designers, and 3-D designers.

Case Study–

Dwango, an acronym for Dial-up Wide Area Network Gaming Operation, is a 24 hour gaming network with game servers in major metropolitan cities across the U.S. and Canada. The Houston, Texas-based Dwango **(713-467-8865)** takes the unusual route of selling game server franchises for their network. The company's main drawing card is a proprietary transmission technology that promises to make MPG networked games as fast as CD-ROM and other games that are not networked. Eventually, Dwango will allow users from around the globe to compete against each other on the most current multiplayer games.

Music Makers

Interactive music is a frontier sector that few recording artists have successfully tapped into. Todd Rundgren, an acknowledged leader in this arena, has yet to have his interactive CD-ROM music hit the mainstream. The problem isn't Todd's music, but the music industry itself. That's because the industry doesn't foresee a widespread platform from which users can play interactive music.

While the fate of interactive music is up in the air, there's one music sector in the frontier that's making waves through the recording industry: The home digital recording studio.

☞ NEW OPPORTUNITY

Personal Recording Studios

It's not unusual for professional recording studios to charge several hundreds of dollars for a single hour of time. A commercial jingle or film often calls for an orchestral score consisting of 30 or more musicians. The expense of recording might strike a sour note with upstart bands and others in need of more economical ways of recording.

Fortunately, digital technology has made it possible for musicians and producers to build professional-style recording studios on a slim $5,000 budget. The digital part of the equation is found in a digital audiotape machine for mastering, and a synthesizer for mimicking the sound of practically any musical instrument.

Since sounds can be stored digitally, they are easily downloaded from the Internet (see Chapter 4, On-line Catalogs), purchased via mail order, or created and stored on disk for future use. Several computer programs facilitate digital recording, mixing, and editing of music. All this has led to an estimated 1 million home studios in the U.S.. For musicians looking to compose and score music for multimedia CD-ROMs, as well as for other uses, the opportunity is not only great, but relatively inexpensive.

√√ *MIDI and Synthesized Music*

The desktop recording studio producer described above may very well produce synthesized music that is created using digital technology. With hardware and software protocols called MIDI, or Musical Instrument Digital Interface, musical sounds from a variety of instruments can be sampled and stored in the computer or synthesizer for future use.

MIDI music has gained wide acceptance and is used for prearranged back-up tracks, multimedia music, sound effects, and commercial soundtracks. It's even used as an instructional tool. In other words, the ability to sample diverse musical instruments puts the power of an entire orchestra in the hands of a single MIDI maestro.

Case Study–

Hardware and software products are at the core of the MIDI industry. For example, Yamaha's Digital Musical Instrument Department in Buena Park, California **(800-932-0001)** produces synthesizers that contain their own powerful operating systems, memory, and storage space for MIDI voices, or sounds.

Then there are companies such as Palo Alto, California-based Opcode Systems **(415-856-3333)** that provide software for writing, recording, and playing back MIDI music.

CHAPTER 6

ADVERTISING & MARKETING

"One does not discover new lands without consenting to lose sight of the shore for a very long time."
André Gide

Industry Snapshot

Just when you thought the digital frontier couldn't possibly contain another sector loaded with hype and hyperbole, you land in the advertising and marketing sector. Lucky thing, though. Because whatever your endeavor on the frontier, chances are you'll want to share it, sell it, send it, customer service it, and hype it with gusto.

The digital tools at your disposal here include such

things as E-mail, consumer on-line services, bulletin board services, Internet advertising and publicity, CD-ROMs, and more. If you've worked in advertising, publicity, marketing, and distribution, you've already got the skills necessary to move into the digital frontier. Don't be intimidated by what you'll see here. This is a new medium with some unique attributes and new challenges. And, if this sector puts you into orbit, delve more deeply with Len Keeler's book *Cyber Marketing*.

OCCUPATIONAL OPPORTUNITIES FOR:

- **Ad Agencies/Account Executives**

- **Catalogers**

- **Computer Programmers**

- **Customer Service**

- **Electronic Data Interchange (EDI)**

- **Entrepreneurs**

- **Internet Access Providers**

- **Market Research**

- **Mail Order & Retail Outlets**

- **On-line Services & BBS**

- **Software Engineers**

- **Multimedia Designers**

- **Net Relations (Public Relations)**

- **Publishers**

- **Net Writers (Copy Writers)**

- **Web Page Designers**

As you navigate around this sector, visit the Buy One Get One Free Bazaar where you can always get a deal on personalized promotional items. Company logo mouse pads make for a nice giveaway item here in the digital frontier.

Obviously, there's too much happening in this realm to cover it in one chapter. Still, this overview should give you a sense of the opportunities in marketing and selling on the digital frontier.

Customer Service

If content is king in the on-line world, then customer satisfaction and quality are king and queen in the product world. For proof, look no further than the automotive industry. Two studies from J.D. Power and Associates, the *Initial Quality Survey* (IQS) and *Customer Satisfaction Index* (CSI) are as likely to be known by consumers looking for cars than the pros at the dealership.

For those involved in customer service, imagine the opportunity of setting up Internet customer support for all kinds of products and services. And, you'll be adding value to your current job at the company where you work.

√ *On-line Customer Service & Support*

What better way to demonstrate a commitment to customer satisfaction than by offering the extra convenience of on-line help to valued customers? On-line service provides several benefits. It can be available all hours of the day, and customers don't have to listen to that infuriating busy signal or be put on hold. Also, prices and other information can be updated more quickly and at a lower cost.

For electronic publishers and those familiar with authoring and database programs, on-line customer service means the opportunity to become a provider of on-line documentation and manuals. Best of all, on-line manuals and documentation can be easily downloaded, thereby eliminating the cost of printing and distribution.

Case Study–

The computer software retailer Egghead uses on-line customer service to help customers make better software decisions *before* they buy. Visitors to Egghead's site (**http://www.egghead.com**) are invited to read various magazine reviews of software. They can also garner the opinions of others who are willing to share their software experiences.

The customer support site also helps build a mailing list. Egghead builds its list by offering a 5% discount to all who register to become members of the company's Cue Club. The Web site also contains a built-in help button to support customer E-mail messages and provide information.

Electronic Data Interchange

Here's a huge service industry used by businesses

of all types. If you're interested in getting involved in the kind of business that made Ross Perot what he is today, then read on.

Electronic Data Interchange, or EDI, makes our world run more efficiently, and yet we're barely aware of it. Through EDI, computers exchange information along private and public networks. This is accomplished without reams of paperwork and without much human involvement.

√√ *Electronic Data Interchange*

Is EDI what happens when you buy something over your computer via a credit card purchase? Yes, but it's actually much more sophisticated than that. Strictly speaking, Electronic Data Interchange is the means by which high volume transactions between companies and other trading partners occur. Here's how.

Networked computers keep track of inventory. When that inventory gets low, purchase orders are automatically generated to replenish the supply. The system goes so far as to include information on how much is to be shipped and where it is to be sent.

In addition to helping reduce paperwork, EDI offers the advantage of immediacy in knowing what products are moving faster off the shelves and being able to respond more quickly to what the market wants.

Case Study–

Traditionally, EDI service providers such as MCI's EDI Net Services **(800-999-2096)**, General Electric's EDI Express **(800-EDI-KNOW)**, and AT&T EDI **(800-242-6005)**, have linked up industry-specific EDI partners and participants. If EDI is developed on the Internet, it could become an affordable tool used by many business.

Through Internet EDI, a company's buyer or computer system will search the net for suppliers of almost any product, service, or even a mailing list. A request for price quotes will be electronically sent. Then, after a buyer approves a particular quote, ordering, invoicing, and even payment will be made through EDI technology.

Although a universal EDI system is not yet available on the Internet, the time may come when this powerful business and marketing tool will be a reality. For entrepreneurs and programmers wanting to know more, try contacting the Alexandria, Virginia-based Data Interchange Standards Association, Inc. **(703-548-7005)**.

Interactive Advertising, Marketing, & Distribution

In combination, the Web, on-line services, and CD-ROM allow for as many ways of reaching niche markets as any other contemporary means. For advertising account executives, copywriters, artists, graphic designers, PR specialists, merchandisers, and others, this new interactive medium is a cornucopia of opportunity.

Advertising is a quarter of a trillion dollar a year industry, worldwide. Jingles, TV ads, radio spots, and print ads must be working, otherwise businesses wouldn't be investing millions each year on advertising for everything from cereal to cars.

New media organizations like the Interactive Marketing Institute **(202-624-7372)** explore interactive advertising's many shapes and forms.

First and foremost, there's the Internet, which is capable of making millions of connections through

Web pages, E-mail, and newsgroups.

Next, there are the major consumer on-line services. Each has its own style and pricing for advertising. CompuServe, which originally eschewed advertising except for limited special events, plans on making advertising accessible through a "services" menu on the welcome screen, as well as on a Web advertising site. Prodigy, on the other hand, makes ads conspicuous by placing them on most screens. America Online's more subtle approach allows for sponsorship in conjunction with selected content, as well as a Web browser link to a dedicated Web advertising site.

Then there are CD-ROMs, which give advertisers a true multimedia interface combining text, video and graphics. Product demos on CD-ROM catalogs make buying decisions easy. Ordering is even easier.

A touch of an on-screen button automatically dials your phone and hooks you up with the computerized order desk on the other end of the line. America Online, one of the pioneers of CD-ROM shopping, places products from several retail store catalogs on its *2 Market* interactive shopping service CD-ROM **(800-622-6600)**. (For more information on interactive retailing and catalogs, see Chapters 2 & 4.)

☞ NEW OPPORTUNITY

Interactive Ad Agency

With the Internet and the World Wide Web, any company can advertise its wares. But why do it yourself when an interactive ad agency specializes in this medium?

Interactive ad agencies will provide the following services. They will set up an interactive Web store front designed to attract qualified customers and leads. The agency will help build an awareness of your business through various newsgroups and E-mail. They will publish and distribute all kinds of relevant information about your business and products, including electronic press releases, brochures, newsletters, and catalogs.

In addition, the interactive ad agency will evaluate your on-line competition. More importantly, the agency can conduct extensive market research and maintain data about your company's performance on the Web site. This data might include E-mail lists, a tabulation of what visitors to your site seem to like the best, and how much time they spend at any one area in your site. The agency's account executive will also make sure that sites are current, updated, and interesting places to visit.

Some Web-zines or cyber zines are now experimenting with flat fee ad rates based on the number of user impressions.

√√ *Advertising on Consumer On-line Services*

If you have a product to advertise, consumer on-line services provide several means of reaching your market. There are classifieds sections and specialized malls or storefronts that link with the Internet. The major consumer on-line services all provide various methods for making advertising accessible.

Why go through a consumer on-line service to get to the Internet when it's not necessary? One compelling reason is greater traffic. On-line services are like being located in what is basically a large mall, as opposed to a small store in some faraway part of town. In some cases, this may help you reach a larger audience consisting of both World Wide Web users plus on-line subscribers.

And then there's the "more" factor. The more consumers use the on-line services, the more services they want. Once users get into the habit of obtaining information over the computer, they'll want all the other conveniences it can offer, from buying their airline tickets to purchasing electronics gear, and so on.

Case Study–

America Online's *Downtown AOL* **(800-615-4127)** reaches both Internet users on the Web, plus AOL's regular subscribers. AOL's marketing demographics can be downloaded by going to the site's webmaster **(webmaster@downtown.web.aol.com)**.

The main screen resembles a mall with stores arranged in categories that include advertising, automotive, books, catalogs, employment, jewelry, printing, sports, clothing, entertainment, gifts, professional services, travel, audio and video, education, flowers and florists, and insurance, to name a few.

What does it cost? A yearly rate for a basic text screen costs less than $500. There are add-on options for graphics, linking to other areas in the document and other Web sites, file downloads, and other extras.

Microsoft Network plans on selling billboards with an advertiser's name, which would link to that advertiser's Internet Web site. The asking price is $7,500 per month with a year long commitment.

Prodigy's advertising links Web billboards to an advertiser's home page. Advertising placement rates depend on the location of the icon or billboard. For Prodigy's Web reference list or other prime locations, rates range from $250 to $1,000 or more per week.

√√ *Customized Web Marketing Software*

Suppose you have a unique agricultural product that appeals to very distinct markets. For example, assume these distinct markets are comprised of restaurant chefs, food technologists, and grocery chains. Rather than use a shotgun approach that gives all three groups the same message, imagine how much more effective it would be if you could tailor that message for each one.

Fortunately, as a savvy Web developer, interactive marketer, or ad agency, you'll have a few software tricks up your proverbial sleeve that will enable you to do the tailoring. For software developers who understand the needs of advertisers on the Web, these opportunities will belong to them as well.

Case Study–

W3.COM (415-323-3378 & http://www.w3.com) is a Palo Alto, California-based software developer that designs specialized marketing tools for the Web. The company's Web Site Toolkit offers functions for counting a site's users, tracking movement of users through a site, and tailoring messages according to certain user E-mail ID extensions.

This ability to differentiate lets Web sites deliver home pages and messages designed especially for a niche market. W3.COM offers its affordable software as a turnkey package for those wanting more advanced marketing tools.

152

☞ NEW OPPORTUNITY

On-Line Ratings

The television industry has the Nielsen Ratings. It won't be long before the on-line medium has an audience-style rating system of its own.

The need exists. All you have to do is compare advertising rates on Web-zines, Web sites, and on-line services, and you're likely to find some wide pricing discrepancies. How do you know what's fair? What's a bargain? What exactly are you paying for, anyway?

Monitoring rating standards is the Coalition for Advertising Supported Information and Entertainment (http//www.commercepark. com/AAA/bc/casie/guide.html).

As tracking and audience rating systems develop, ad rates will be based on what should be very accurate measurements. Among the newest group of high-tech companies creating on-line ratings is San Francisco, California-based Internet Profiles Corporation (415-975-5800).

Auditing technology, like that from Internet Profiles and others, will give companies the assurance that there are tools to measure their exposure. Measurements will include items like the number of users visiting a site, a count of downloads, and the time spent in specific areas.

If you're an advertiser, stay tuned. These impending rating standards will open up a digital world of interactive advertising opportunities for yourself and your clients.

√√ *Advertising on Content Sites*

There are different places to advertise on-line. These include the World Wide Web, consumer on-line services, electronic BBS systems, and at a content site. Content, whether it consists of on-line magazines, information archives, or on-line entertainment, may provide the best demographics, strongest presence, and compelling interactivity. And while it may cost more, it may end up being more valuable in the long run.

Sponsorship within a content site creates a powerful link between the content site and the advertiser. In the early days of TV, many programs were sponsored. That stopped when the networks discovered they could sell spot advertising for more than the cost of producing their own programs.

Sure, it makes sense for computer-related products to advertise on-line because the products are directly reaching computer users. (How else could they be on-line?)

Fortunately, people who use computers have other interests. And they can be reached via content since that's the reason they came on-line in the first place. The case study below illustrates how products that have nothing to do with computers can reach a market through on-line sponsorship of high quality content.

Case Study–

InterZine Productions **(203-226-4808)**, a Westport,

Connecticut-based on-line and Internet production company, developed the interactive golfing site *iGOLF*. With its own area on America Online, *iGOLF* appeals to golfers through a unique blend of original writings from experts, up-to-date tournament information, profiles and rankings of professional players, golf related stocks, and contests.

The demographics for *iGOLF* aren't too hard to figure out. It reaches two expanding markets– the on-line user and golfer. Not surprisingly, Callaway Golf, a maker of golf clubs, is one of the area's primary sponsors. As a sponsor, Callaway gets featured on *iGOLF's* main menu screen. Callaway's area is also interactive, featuring golf tips from Johnny Miller, Callaway's new catalog, late-breaking golf news, and more.

Who sells sponsorships or finds advertisers for on-line areas? Anyone with sales experience can. Here's an especially good opportunity for TV and magazine media reps to sell existing clients on digital frontier marketing, usually at a fraction of the cost of TV.

√√ *Interactive Card Decks*

If you're a direct marketer, you'll know we're not talking about playing cards here. Card decks are one of direct marketing's most basic tools. It consists of a deck of cards, often 100 or more, each with an offer or coupon for products or a request for more information. Card decks give companies a relatively low cost way to reach hundreds of thousands of potential customers.

Case Study–

Jericho, NY-based CMP Publications **(516-733-6800)** operates a *Virtual Tech Deck* that does more than give interested customers a card to fill out and a wait of several weeks before receiving information back.

With CMP's Web deck service, customers are instantly linked up to companies that have home pages. If customers simply want information, then the company is E-mailed directly to the advertiser's on-line address.

Web decks, in addition to delivering instantaneous responses, have another major advantage over traditional card decks: Any single card can easily be modified. Web publishing makes for an ideal test environment, and it allows marketers to try different approaches until they find one that works.

TRENDS 2000:

Software Distribution On-line

Just as the on-line distribution of training manuals and documentation makes sense, the trend towards delivering software on-line makes even more sense. After all, here's a case of a digital product being distributed directly into a computer that reads digital information. A perfect match!

Some on-line book publishers allow you to download one chapter of a book to sample. Likewise, some game developers let you download limited versions of their games to try before you buy.

The most dramatic new trend of all, however, appears to be that of networked computing from home workstations.

Software will be downloaded only as long as it is needed for a particular task, but will remain stored on a remote location. You'll pay for software as you need it– by the minute or the hour!

Consider that if this happens, we won't need all the potent processing power that resides in today's computers. Instead, a class of computers will be designed solely for on-line Internet and Web access. Oracle Systems Corporation, among others, are developing these network-only computers.

Net Relations

Like public relations, those specializing in net relations do a little bit of everything. If you're a technological evangelist who is net savvy, then you'll be well suited to this line of work. It includes getting businesses and people digital, from helping them get a Web home page to helping them with their content.

Net relations addresses a number of digital frontier issues about how to use the new medium. This can be translated into the question: How do you bring people to your Web page and make money?

In net relations, you'll need to know the geographic landscape of the Internet so you can advise on the best place to situate a Web page. There are technical considerations, too, such as using the right mix of graphics and text, as well as the right compression tools, to make a Web site accessible and fun to use.

The PR Newswire **(800-832-5522)** is one example of a turnkey operation specializing in electronic PR distribution to all the major wire services. On the Web **(http://www.prnewswire.com)**, however, it offers no major electronic Internet PR distribution. As Web sites proliferate, such a service business will be viable and offer significant growth potential.

☞ **NEW JOB AREA**

Net Relations Specialist

Do you have what it takes to be a pioneer in the new field of (Inter)Net Relations? You just might if: You know your way around Internet newsgroups and the Web like the back of your hand; you've got journalistic credentials with excellent writing skills and have worked in marketing, advertising, or PR; you understand enough about data compression, transmission speeds, and other technology to be dangerous; you know your way around a news release and are a wizard at organizing events and making contacts.

*Miller/Shandwick Technologies (**617-536-0470 &**), with offices in Boston, London, Silicon Valley, Dallas, and Los Angeles, specializes in net relations and has a home page (**http://www.millercom.com**) dedicated to the Internet. The company offers whole programs designed for technology-based firms.*

Net specialists will use new tools, such as software that scans the Web, monitoring everything from newsgroups to E-mail lists.

*InfoSeek, a Santa Clara, California-based company (**http://www2.infoseek.com**), offers these same services through its Net Search.*

Net relations is an excellent example of how the digital frontier needs to be populated to accomplish what's been done before, only with a new set of technological skills.

☞ NEW JOB AREA

Web Link Artist

This job will exist, but it's so new that the job title could be almost anything, from Linking Engineer to Web Link Artist. Before you come up with your own suitable moniker, let's look at a job description as it might appear in the classifieds some day in the not too distant future.

"Wanted: Web linking specialist to connect technology-oriented, hot new Web site to more of the same. Must be fluent in all Web search engines, able to make programming links through Netscape tools, and use PageMaker to create and design graphics for links on our site. Will pay $ for every new link."

Finding sites to link to takes a lot of time and thought. The more popularized Web sites become, the more discriminating owners of sites will grow. The quality of links will be

159

more important than quantity, and the job will require someone with good sales skills.

☞ NEW JOB AREA

Mail List Cruiser

This job is the cousin of the Web Link Artist, but is more specialized. So, what exactly do Mail List Cruisers do? They surf the Internet searching for mailing lists on which to place soft sell PR. Here's how it works:

Suppose you've already done your PR blitz to the usual cadre of magazines, newspapers, cyber magazines, and so on. Now, you need to get word out in a more subtle way, but aimed directly at individuals in your target audience. How do you achieve this lofty goal? With the services of Mail List Cruisers.

First, here's the skinny on E-mail lists. The Internet is crammed with thousands of newsgroups and mailing lists. Anyone can "subscribe" to a list for free. Once on a list, subscribers are sent copies of messages that have been posted, or placed, on the mailing list's computer server. As soon as new postings are made, they are distributed automatically to all the list's subscribers.

If you're interested in checking out marketing-oriented lists, you might try subscribing to direct marketing lists such as

160

*Directmar **(majordomo@world.std.com)**, or Inet-Marketing **(listproc@einet.net)**.*

*Mail List Cruisers need to identify the right list for a PR posting. One listserv which contains many lists is **majordomo@world. std.com**. From this listserv, you'll see how lists are an essential tool for sending and receiving information.*

Internet list subscribers, however, are wary of blatant selling. Anyone who misuses a list may end up being flamed with hundreds of messages.

*One company that judiciously uses Internet savvy college students for part-time cruising is Quality Media Resources, Inc. **(206-455-0558)**. The Bellevue, Washington-based business produces corporate-themed videos relating to issues like leadership, diversity in the workplace, management, and quality.*

The company uses Mail List Cruisers to locate groups interested in training, equal employment opportunity, employee support issues, organizational change, management development, and organizational learning. Then, the cruisers post a "message" that discusses the topic and follows with a contact number for anyone wanting more information.

If you're interested in becoming a Mail List Cruiser, put word of your services out to on-line ad agencies and PR companies. Or, start your own cruising company by contacting businesses the old fashioned way (by phone or mail) and let them know what you can do for them.

CHAPTER 7

VIRTUAL REALITY

"Success comes from taking the path of maximum advantage instead of the path of least resistance."
George Bernard Shaw

Industry Snapshot

Remember the commercial that asked, "Is it real, or is it Memorex?" The virtual reality outpost could go one better by asking, "Why settle for reality when you can have virtual reality?"

No one in this outpost dares to contend that virtual reality is a mature industry. It's still passing through an awkward adolescence, and proud of it. This outpost is an exploratory one. If there were a Digital Extreme Sports Competition, then virtual reality would be the most extreme and far out. Get the picture?

If you decide to tackle a job or opportunity here, be prepared to spend about half your time describing what it is that you do. First, if you're going to spend time in this outpost, you need to understand the difference between virtual reality (also known as VR) and multimedia.

Multimedia, by and large, consists of a prestored and predetermined set of graphics, text, video, music, and sound. Much of virtual reality, by contrast, is made up of visual databases with images being created, modeled, and textured at that moment.

Like any other area, you needn't be an expert in VR to find a job in the area. You may find an application that's ideally suited to your line of work.

OCCUPATIONAL OPPORTUNITIES FOR:

- **Actors**

- **Architects**

- **Artists**

- **Computer Programmers**

- **Computer Repair Technicians**

- **Entrepreneurs**

- **Game Developers**

- **Marketing Staff**

- **Photographers**

- **Psychologists**

- **Public Relations Specialists**

- **Product Designers and Managers**

- **Set Designers & Lighting Designers**

- **Simulation Developers**

- **Software Engineers**

- **Systems Engineers and Analysts**

- **Video Game Technicians**

- **Web Publishers**

If VR seems ephemeral, its applications are for real. Ask anyone at the Smoke & Mirrors Pub for a demo of the latest HMD (Head Mounted Display) and your head will be swimming with ideas for jobs and opportunities like those that follow!

Arts & Entertainment

By virtue of its ability to transport us into other worlds, virtual reality is making great strides in entertainment. From digital art galleries to arcade games, VR's entertainment applications are diverse.

√√ *Art Galleries*

You don't have to be a digital artist to appreciate the possibilities for transforming almost any kind of art into a digital form. As if to prove this point, digital art

165

galleries present several kinds of art. Some are even interactive, with images that change when the viewer stands in front of a computer screen.

Case Study–

Virtual art exhibits and galleries make it possible for visitors to go on-line and experience art. The Kinetic Gallery (**http://www.win.net/~kinetic**) gives visitors a close-up look at scanned artwork. The gallery also includes biographies of artists and information on pricing and ordering.

Are there jobs here? You bet. For example, you could create a Web site that indexes all the different art galleries, sign up artists to create your own virtual gallery, or even design Web pages for artists and galleries that want to get exposure.

√√ Games & Arcades

A whole new generation of dedicated, virtual reality game machines is underway. Sega, Nintendo, Atari, and Silicon Graphics are just some of the major product developers in this burgeoning area.

But while the home VR game develops, the multi-billion dollar a year theme park industry is entrenched and actively using VR to compete for customers. Virtual reality attractions up the excitement value by adding a powerful new arsenal of thrills to theme parks and arcades.

Shopping mall developers, hungry for action, are snapping up new VR games to get people out of the home and back into their malls. These circumstances are good news for game developers, computer programmers, marketers, game testers, video game technicians, and arcade managers.

Case Study–

Virtual World Entertainment **(213-625-8484)**, a Los Angeles-based company, specializes in high-tech and virtual reality amusement. With stores located in major urban centers throughout the U.S., Australia, and Japan, the company's virtual reality computer games give the average gamer a chance to take on a completely different reality and persona.

Mega malls with virtual reality entertainment centers are opening around the U.S.. Traditional movie theaters will be supplemented by 3-D theaters and simulation rides giving viewers a sense of movement.

Another firm forging ahead with VR entertainment centers is Blockbuster Entertainment Group **(800-827-4955)**. The Ft. Lauderdale, Florida-based video rental chain has introduced its "Block Party" entertainment centers featuring a host of VR rides and games. You'll also find simulation theater rides that will shake, rattle, and roll you in sync with a video image.

☞ NEW JOB AREA

Virtual Actor

Imagine slipping into a full body suit of cyber clothing and gloves that are wired up to a computer. Every move you make is tracked, registered spatially, and sent to the computer where thousands of calculations are made. The information is transmitted real time to a digital comic character. The character, who is on a TV screen, moves in sync with you like an identical twin.

167

Your digital Doppelganger even opens his mouth when you do, speaking your words. Though no one outside the digital studio has seen you perform, you are a virtual actor.

This new form of acting will become more predominant over time, especially as its cost drops below that of traditional and computer animation. And the stage background? It may be that of a virtual set (see below).

√√ *Virtual Set Design*

There is good reason why newcomers to set design should spend more time working on the computer than in wood shop. Graphic designers, architects, and those with computer aided design backgrounds will take the lead in developing the sets of the future.

If you've ever visited a film or television studio, then you know that soundstages take up a lot of real estate. When videotaping and filming are not taking place, soundstages are often left empty. Serialized programs like soap operas, for example, may have as many as 100 different sets. It costs a lot in terms of material and labor to build sets, not to mention the time spent striking and storing them.

Many problems associated with sets can be solved with virtual set design. By using computer-modeled sets, design and size constraints become irrelevant. Virtual sets are ideal for game shows, soap operas, news, special events, and sports. And, since several virtual sets can be stored on computer at the same time, it's easy to switch between sets as needed.

Case Study–

A San Francisco-based company that's leading the

new broadcast paradigm of virtual sets is Electrogig **(415-956-8212 & http://www.electrogig.com)**. The company even helped create a major segment of ABC's program *20/20* featuring John Stassel which utilized a virtual set.

Once a virtual set is created, actors moving through the set are tracked so that they are able to interact with it and literally move behind, through, or in front of the set's elements.

Different cameras treat the set as a three dimensional space, and even zooming the camera in or out will change the set's perspective. And it's easy to give any virtual set a new look, color, or texture.

☞ NEW JOB AREA

Virtual Set & Lighting Designer

Virtual set designers are graphic design specialists who understand computer modeling tools, which are an extension of Computer Aided Design. Currently, sets are modeled and colored using existing programs like Photoshop. Once the virtual set is built, you can have your actors or talent "walk through" it and see how it all looks.

Virtual set design can also be used to simply model a set before actually constructing it. At the University of Kansas, stage designs are built on computer before being built on stage. This eliminates the need for scale models because virtual set information can be used to create blueprints. More importantly, virtual stage design lets the designer check sight lines from various seating perspectives!

Virtual lighting designers will find new jobs as a result of this new technology. Lighting is a key element of any production. Virtual lighting allows several lighting effects to be tried out. Once lighting is chosen, it has to be matched in the studio whenever live actors are involved. If the actor interacts with the virtual set, then this becomes an even greater issue.

Traditional lighting designers can learn these new skills by working with the virtual set designer. The day will come when there will be those who will specialize in virtual lighting design both in the computer and on the live set.

☞ NEW JOB AREA

Virtual Architect

Why settle for a scale model or rendition of your new home when you can take a stroll through a virtual model? Architects now use computer aided design programs which permit them to "walk through" a virtual space and see how it feels before building it.

Virtual architects will use 3-D modeling tools to give those who are renovating or designing a new home a realistic sense of proportion and size. The virtual home can even be furnished with models of your existing or ideal furnishings to get a better idea of space and flow.

And if there are virtual architects, why not virtual interior designers? Such a designer will one day let you try out furniture and art in a model of your virtual home before you decide to buy it!

TRENDS 2000:

Virtual Objects

On ABC's 20/20 program where John Stassel moved through a virtual set, he interacted with a small podium. The podium was a real object, but in the future, actors will be able to interact virtual objects.

With what is called virtual reality collision course objects, an actor's path will collide with virtual objects, causing them to move. Actors will be able to pick them up, put them down, and generally treat them as if they were the real thing.

If you thought video could be manipulated to alter reality, digital technologies like virtual sets and objects can go a step farther. Imagine, if you will, a crime scene or disaster area. It's already possible to have reporters "dropped in" and move around these scenes as if they were really there.

Political rallies and other events could be virtually created and managed to make them deliver the wanted effect. Certainly, this raises ethical issues. News and other broadcast events are certain to come under scrutiny as these virtual techniques become commonplace.

☞ NEW OPPORTUNITY

Virtual Photo Store

At shopping malls, we've all seen the cut-outs of famous people and backgrounds of famous places that we can be photographed next to. This decidedly low-tech approach will eventually be replaced with virtual locations.

Want to send a virtual video of yourself interacting (or acting) with Marilyn Monroe? Or meeting with President Kennedy a la Tom Hanks in the movie Forrest Gump? *How about a video of you and the kids vacationing in the Bahamas?*

This kind of shopping mall attraction is on the horizon. It's only a matter of time until it will all be possible on a small soundstage.

Business

Virtual reality offers business some valuable services. Executives and managers will use a new set of virtual tools for conveying their ideas, selling products and services, and distributing work.

You might not find a VR job or career in the Sunday classified section. But what might help your job hunting is an ability to write code, a knowledge of the latest VR trends, and high visibility at VR conferences. With a yearning for learning, you're sure to reach into the following areas and beyond.

√√ *Virtual Sales Presentations*

Sales people are forever searching for better tools to help sell their wares. Video presentations that describe corporate capabilities have been a valuable commodity for many years. Now, however, interactive CD-ROM multimedia sales presentations on laptop computers (Chapter 3) deliver a more flexible, potent sales tool.

Interactive VR presentations have their own strengths. They are especially suited to modeling physical layouts in a realistic way.

Case Study–
One company utilizing virtual reality as a sales tool is Amsco International, Inc., an Erie, Pennsylvania-based health care equipment company. Amsco sales reps use a laptop computer that runs real-time interactive layouts showing its health care equipment in a virtual medical environment. With this kind of VR sales tool, customers can immediately visualize any design. The goal? Shortening the sales process while at the same time aiding in decision making.

Summit Graphics **(412-854-5076)**, a Bethel Park, Pennsylvania-based 3-D animation and virtual reality developer creates presentations like the one Amsco uses. Summit Graphics also built a virtual steel mill for Samsung and Tippons companies. The virtual mill was shown to steel engineers during a trade show.

√/ *Virtual Office Parks*

What is a virtual office park? Like a real office park, it is a collection of businesses sharing some of the same services and space. The difference is that those shared services are not the local Roach Coach on wheels, but high-speed, networked digital transmission capabilities. The shared space is not a gated driveway into an industrial park, but a disk farm offering terabyte upon terabyte of file storage.

There are other advantages, too. Businesses in a virtual office park increase the opportunity of meeting and providing services to each other.

Case Study–

Pacific Bell **(800-408-PARK)** developed the idea of building new media business parks with the hope of bringing together users and creators of multimedia content. Pacific Bell's trial media park, initiated in 1994, offers three different levels of access, including ISDN, T-1, and DS-3 lines. High speed access makes it possible to store and retrieve files that reside on a disk farm with terabytes of disk space. It's no different from renting a warehouse and eliminates storage of digital files on-site.

Those participating in the trial media park included an on-line talent agency, a stock film and video company, a multimedia producer, musician Herbie Hancock, Apple Computer, a stock music library, a post production company, and Paramount Productions.

If you or your company should need to purchase any equipment in order to join the virtual office park, the phone company is only too happy to offer one-stop shopping.

√√ *Virtual Training*

The military has been using virtual reality for tank and flight training for many years. Finally, the rest of the training world is realizing the benefits. That's great news for the instructional designers and simulation developers who will lead the way in creating the next generation of VR computer based training.

Virtual reality training lets users learn through using software that simulates the experience of using an actual device or application. So essentially, it is another form of computer based training.

The difference is that VR training can let you learn by making mistakes. Just like in real life. There are still prompts and messages that guide you, but the virtual reality simulation provides a degree of freedom not always found in many other kinds of computer based training.

Case Study–

Emultek Ltd. **(203-891-8495)** is a Connecticut-based business that develops virtual reality simulation software which is used in computer based training applications. For example, Emultek's software, *Rapid*, was used to create the computer based virtual training simulation for the Magellan NAV 1000 GPS navigation system.

In addition to its use in commercial aviation, virtual reality training simulations are the only reliable way of training pilots to use advanced planes like Lockheed's

F-22 fighter. The plane's display technology resembles a video arcade shooting game.

Military simulation developers stretch the limits of virtual training in other ways. The latest training simulations utilize multiplayer battlefield conditions complete with virtual enemies and futuristic weapons that aren't even built yet.

Medicine

Virtual medicine promises to deliver better quality of care, as well as some novel approaches to treating illness. These new techniques may also help reduce healthcare costs at the same time.

The new opportunities being made available include the areas of digital imaging, simulation development, and software development.

√√ *Virtual Diagnosis & Virtual Surgery*

Physicians often get X-rays or CAT-scans that show things they are unfamiliar with. But for doctors in small towns, getting a second opinion from an expert is not always the easiest thing to do. And, it takes a lot of time. Fiber optic links between hospitals and labs are changing all that.

Getting an instant second opinion from an expert 3,000 miles away will be as routine as driving to your local clinic. It's especially promising for distant rural areas that lack advanced medical services. By adding satellite links, this kind of virtual diagnosis service could be expanded to a global basis.

Virtual surgery, on the other hand, uses simulation training to let doctors practice difficult surgeries on a 3-D image of a patient. They'll get to operate with virtual scalpels and lasers before doing it for real.

Case Study–

At UCLA Medical Center, digital images of everything from ultrasounds to CAT-scans are transmitted all the way from a Florida lab for review by UCLA specialists. This is just one example of technology that didn't exist a short time ago.

√√ *Virtual Psychotherapy*

One of the things that virtual reality does best is model perspectives in relation to the head movement of the user. This is accomplished with head mounted displays that immerse the user in a visual field capable of representing almost any image.

Clinicians and researchers are thus asking: Why not tailor an immersive image to help treat behavioral disorders? To that end, virtual reality is being used to treat acrophobia, which is a fear of heights.

Normally, therapists treat acrophobia by taking patients on excursions outside the office where they can overcome their fears in real life. VR therapy saves time because it lets the subject undergo therapy in the doctor's office, while providing the same degree of control over the behavioral conditioning process.

Virtual therapy may help provide relief from a wide variety of phobias by using realistic scenes that are difficult to find outside the doctor's office.

Case Study–

Georgia Institute of Technology is one of the first to experiment with VR psychotherapy. By using a head mounted display, or HMD, acrophobics view images that produce anxiety by placing the subject on a bridge, a high balcony, and even an open glass elevator.

The process is no different than that used for most behavioral conditioning. Subjects begin at low anxiety producing levels, then slowly move higher once they become comfortable with a particular height and situation. All the subjects in the school's study mastered the high anxiety producing environments.

TRENDS 2000:

Mind Controlled Computers

You want to play a computer game or type a message in your computer. But instead of touching the keyboard or mouse, you look at the monitor and simply think about moving the cursor to a new position. Think again, and the cursor clicks on a menu or icon.

Is this a new sci-fi idea? Some new virtual reality game? Or is it really happening?

It's really happening. Enroll in any brain physiology class and you'll learn that the brain generates electrical activity, be it ever so small.

It's a matter of training ourselves to create different brain waves that are read by electrodes attached to the head. These waves can then be used to trigger cursor movements.

This and other technologies like it will impact disabled persons who cannot easily move or speak. Researchers from Boston College's Project Eagle Eye are using eye movement to direct cursor movement.

Sausalito, California-based The Other 90% Technologies (415-332-0433) takes another approach. It has developed a finger pad to read galvanic skin response. This is the same kind of technology used by lie detectors.

The company already offers a number of mind control programs for use with PCs. Games include MindSkier, MindMusic, *and* MindArt. *There are also personal health and improvement programs for enhancing memory, concentration, and creativity. There's even one called* The Zone *which helps users attain and maximize their mental, emotional, and physical states.*

Eventually, the ability to use brain waves in multiplayer gaming networks and other applications will become reality. While these technologies are leading edge, the opportunity to explore and develop the next generation of mind controlled computers is happening today.

On-line

Virtual reality fits the on-line environment like a hand fits a glove. To start with, if you're on-line you are part of a virtual community, are you not? But VR goes beyond a virtual chatfest and into the transformation of the on-line world from a two-dimensional to a three-dimensional one.

3-D images will enhance several aspects of being on-line. Not only will it make the Internet more welcoming, warm, and fuzzy, but in terms of being a powerful sales tool, 3-D capability is a bonanza. For example, how useful would it be to see your view to the stage from any set of theater seats before buying them?

VRML, Virtual Reality Modeling Language, is a new protocol that is giving the net a 3-D facelift. The many new Internet Web sites modeled with VRML will let users navigate and explore in three-dimensional space, faraway places as close as their computer.

Learning VRML is a start for those wanting to prospect in this new sector of the frontier. What follows are just a few of the coming jobs and opportunities on this, the digital frontier's outermost fringe.

√√ *3-D Programmable Objects*

3-D models of objects created in virtual reality modeling language can be used by Web developers. An object could be programmed with multiple layers of information. The object represents a gateway to obtain data or navigate through 3-D space.

Opportunities are there for those who package 3-D programmable objects into a catalog resembling clip art. Only *this* catalog of art is preprogrammed to be functional and usable by Web page designers.

Case Study–

A Woodstock, NY-based software developer, Paper Software Inc. **(914-679-2440 & www.paperinc.com),** offers a 3-D globe of earth which can be mapped with multiple data layers and hypertext links by Web page designers. Need a weather map? Paper Software's globe can do the trick by mapping interactive geographical weather systems at specific locations on the image.

News services, sports, weather, and travel are just a few of the many potential ways to use the 3-D virtual globe. There are other ways to simulate three-dimensions on the Internet. As the next following job area shows, 3-D imaging can be used by almost anyone.

One company offers a catalog full of *CyberProps* and *CyberSets*. 3Name3D **(310-314-2171 & http://www. ywd.com)** is a Santa Monica, California-based firm that develops and sells a line of ready-to-use, off-the-shelf objects. These objects enable multimedia and on-line Web developers to fill their virtual worlds with a host of 3-D props and sets. No muss, no fuss.

√√ *Virtual Photography*

If a picture is worth a thousand words, then a virtual 3-D picture must be worth a million. A flat image is fine for a brochure, but if you're on the Internet the medium begs for more.

The quality of a visual experience is enhanced when the user can manipulate objects or products, and navigate through a virtual space. For example, virtual travelers can stroll through a hotel lobby and check out a suite; virtual students applying to a university can visit the dorm and other sites; virtual shoppers can manipulate products and walk through store aisles.

To make it happen requires some VR technology in combination with either 35mm photography or a video camera. The opportunities and jobs here will go to Web developers and virtual photo studios that make this enhanced 3-D capability available.

Case Study–

View 360 Productions (**martyk@earthlink.net**) is a Los Angeles-based photo studio that specializes in virtual reality photography. Using Kodak's Photo CD, Apple's Virtual Reality developers kit, and QuickTime VR (**http://qtvr.quicktime.apple.com**), View 360 Productions goes to real locations where it plans the photo shoot and photographs the site.

Two rooms, for example, are shot in a panoramic fashion. All the various photos are "stitched" together to create a seamless image which a user can navigate through and around. This process requires not just a photographer, but programmer's touch. Objects in a room, such as a book, can be designated as interactive "hot spots" that link the user to other areas or allow the book to be picked up and looked at in greater detail.

☞ NEW JOB AREA

Virtual Photographer & Photo Studio

If you're a photographer who is used to the logistical nightmare of shooting weddings and anniversaries, you should get the hang of shooting virtual photography in no time.

A virtual reality photographer allows the viewer a means of experiencing spatial interactions through the computer. That means photographing a space with movement

182

in mind. To image a single room you'll need to shoot at least 12 images on a 360° circumference with a 15mm lens and level camera mount.

If there's a coffee mug on a table, then you'll shoot it with the intent of manipulating it like a real object. To accomplish this, you'll move the camera around the object every 10° on two axes and shoot over 70 images.

When you're done, the developed pictures will be imported into the computer and stitched together. The end result will be a coffee mug that can be picked up and looked at from all sides. Or inside, just to check and see if there's any coffee left.

Photographers need to learn special skills to design and shoot virtual photography. In addition to understanding virtual logistics, it's helpful for you to learn Photoshop or other image programs that help fix flaring and other VR photographic problems.

Then, when you're an expert at this new medium, you can sell your services as a Virtual Wedding Photographer. There have already been virtual weddings, so why not virtual wedding photography?

SECTION II

NETWORKING
RESOURCE GUIDE

RESOURCE 1

ON-LINE JOB SEARCH; GOVERNMENT INFO

Introduction to the Resource Guide

Welcome to the springboard for your real-time journey into the digital frontier. As you're about to find, there's a whole cast of helpful resources, both on-line and off-line, aimed at helping you pinpoint gainful employment and opportunities. First, identify those digital frontier areas or chapters that appeal to you the most, (software, hardware, on-line, etc.). Then, go to that chapter's corresponding resource chapter in the Networking Resource Guide. It's that simple.

Resource chapters contain valuable information that will get you up to speed in your chosen area. Associations, publications, conferences, and training are the four cornerstones of networking in the frontier.

Don't be shy about using the resources here. While it would be overload to list all the resources for any one area, these invariably will lead you to others. And others.

Search with a sense of discovery, for the digital frontier has no boundaries but those we ourselves impose!

On-line Job Search

There's a whole cast of helpful on-line sources aimed at helping you find gainful employment and opportunities. The on-line digital frontier has new developments shaping up every day as more and more companies go on-line. Many of these have their own job line. Checking out businesses one by one, however, is an inefficient use of the frontier's tools. Instead, optimize your time by using the following on-line services designed to help expand your horizons.

√√ *Career/NET*

If you want to be on a CD-ROM database tailored to recruiters looking for new college graduates, Career/NET **(800-760-4021)** is that service. A service of I/NET Inc., a Kalamazoo, Michigan-based firm, Career/NET's CD-ROMS are updated throughout the year and contain a variety of detailed information about students.

Students enter their data onto disks provided by Career/NET. This includes a one page personal expression relating to career goals, major, minors, computer skills, languages, activities, GPA, and more. The result is a standardized resume that can be sorted by Career/NET recruiter subscribers.

√√ *careerWEB*

The Internet job search known as careerWEB on the Internet, **http:/www.cweb.com**, is designed to help recruiters, employment managers, and job seekers find one another. The main Web page links to employers, organizations, jobs, career fitness center, professional associations, organizational resources, professional development, and registration.

Norfolk, Virginia-based CareerWEB **(800-871-0800)** focuses on what it calls "high definition" jobs. These are jobs which are specifically tailored to meet the demands of a unique project, advancing technology, and new generation equipment.

One of careerWEB's unusual elements is the ability for recruiters to sift through applications from those who express interest for positions. Job seekers have access to a number of services, including detailed job information, professional associations, opportunities for professional development, career services, and access to an on-line employment service database called Job Bank USA.

Job Bank USA supports the recruitment activity of more than 2,000 businesses, from local to international, and includes all kinds of jobs and skill levels. Employment managers are linked up to over 30,000 Job Bank USA candidates from a range of disciplines, such as alumni organizations, technical associations, and professional associations.

According to Job Bank USA, more than two-thirds of those listed are currently employed but looking for better positions. The service also protects confidentiality when needed.

√√ *Consumer On-line Services*

If you're a subscriber to one of the major consumer on-line services, then you've got numerous job and career services close at hand. One of the more comprehensive packages is available through America Online **(703-448-8700)**. Once logged on to AOL, the Career Center is located through the keyword: **career**.

Almost all of the services in the Career Center are included in the basic monthly subscription price, such as federal government employment opportunities, a searchable resume and talent bank, self-employment guidance, home business kits, help wanted ads collected from the federal government and E-span, and several searchable job databases. One feature, called Help Wanted USA, offers over 10,000 electronic job listings each week.

Placing an electronic resume in the Career Center's on-line database is free, and it's made available to employment and recruitment services. You can even get free career counseling and guidance through three very different approaches, including private on-line counseling, a self-paced instructional program, and a computerized analysis.

The Career Center contains an on-line database, the Hoover's Business Resources database, which is also found on CompuServe, LEXIS/NEXIS, eWorld, and other on-line services. With it, users can search wealth of information found in Hoover's Handbooks.

Hoover's Handbooks, published by Austin-based The Reference Press **(512-454-7778 & http://www. hoovers.com)**, are available at both libraries and bookstores. The books contain detailed information such as the operations, histories, personnel, financial performance, and contact numbers for thousands of private and public U.S. companies.

√√ *FedWorld*

The government is a prolific publisher. Much of this information is available on-line to those who know where to look. Jobs and opportunities of all kinds are just a modem hookup or phone call away.

FedWorld **(http://fedworld.gov & 703-321-8020)** is a government operated on-line service courtesy of the National Technical Information Service (NTIS). If you wanted to spend hours delving deeper and deeper into over 100 different systems of bulletins boards, here's your chance to get lost. But, if you're interested solely in jobs, you can probably go in and find your way out without too much trepidation.

The government information servers are sorted into main categories. Just go to the index of subject categories, where you'll find job openings listed under the letter J.

If you look hard enough, you'll also find a number of government job contracts available to outside vendors, contractors, and suppliers. Want to do business with the Veterans Administration? There's the VA Vendor BBS. How about the Air Force? You'll want to check out the Air Force Small Business BBS.

The opportunities go on and on. Good luck, and don't forget to come up for air.

√√ *JOBTRAK*

JOBTRAK Corporation **(http://www.jobtrak.com)** is a Los Angeles-based college job listing service. The company is used by over 150,000 employers to fill full and part-time positions. Each day, JOBTRAK places over 500 new jobs on its Internet database.

One of the largest on-line employment services, JOBTRAK **(800-999-8725)** is subscribed to by over 300 major college and university career centers in over 30 different states. The database can be accessed only by students and alumni of these colleges, without charge.

Employers can post a job listing at their choice of colleges, and the cost of the ad depends on the length of the ad and the number of colleges chosen. The ability to target universities saves companies from having to sort through unqualified resumes.

From the job searcher's point of view, there's the ability to research a company profile, study Department of Labor statistics, and even get resume writing tips. In addition to an Internet posting, JOBTRAK's software lets career staff print out hard copies in order to create job bulletins.

√ *JobWeb*

JobWeb (**http://www.jobweb.org**) is the result of the National Association of Colleges and Employers (NACE). Based in Bethlehem, Pennsylvania (**800-544-5272**), this professional association developed JobWeb to meet the career and employment needs of everyone from college students and recent graduates, to college alumni.

Over 1,600 universities and colleges are linked up to JobWeb, making it available to their students and graduates. In addition, there are more than 1,300 employer organizations, from Fortune 500 companies to start-ups, that are represented in JobWeb. The service also includes listings from local, state, and federal government agencies.

JobWeb is a comprehensive job source. The centerpiece of JobWeb is its *Career Directory*, which is a searchable database providing all kinds of employer information.

The *Career Directory* describes companies and links

to current job openings, as well as an organization's own Web home page. Users can respond to job openings by having their database-ready file E-mailed directly to the company and job listing they're interested in. JobWeb also boasts JobPlace, which is described as "one of the nation's largest Internet listservs for career service professionals."

√√ *Mail Lists Servers On-line*

To succeed in any line of work, it helps to know people. Seek out mail listservs and Usenet groups with interests in your line of work. Get to know people, and you might find someone who's looking to hire. You might even post a low key message about your services. Be sure that you become familiar with a Usenet group before posting what could be thought of as an inconsiderate breach of netiquette.

You might even consider getting information from a organizations like EMA, the Employment Management Association **(919-0787-6010)**, or PIHRA, Professionals in Human Resources Association **(213-622-7472)**. These are "member only" organizations, but if you know someone who is a member, you might be able to have them get you a mailing list (there's a fee for this) of the Directors of Human Resources for member companies.

√√ *Monster Board*

The Monster Board **(http://monster.com)** is a job search service that is at the same time both hip and helpful. It has a cool-looking interface which leads users to over 45,000 job listings.

From the home page, you can link to areas like Career Search, Employer Profiles, Resumes On-line,

Career Events, and more. Through Monster's Career Search, you can seek a job by industry, location, discipline, company, or keyword.

The Monster Board also provides some unique services, such as the ROAR Corps, InterNETships, and Resume City. The ROAR Corps is a place where up-and-coming leaders can tap in to the underground world of "flicks, grooves, and prose." Monster offers InterNETships for people wanting to expand their Internet skills. Resume City is an area where HR professionals can go to access the service's database of qualified job seekers.

In addition, the Monster Board links to other useful job services, including Jobs WAIS Search, the Career Center (**www.netline.com/career**), Career Mosaic (**www.careermosaic.com**), and E-Span (**www.espan .com**).

√√ *On-line Classifieds*

Want to search for more employment listings than anywhere on the Web? Try CareerPath.com, a massive collection of classifieds accessible to anyone with a Web browser.

CareerPath.com (**http://www.careerpath.com**) is an interactive, employment service created by six of the nation's largest newspapers: The Boston Globe, Los Angeles Times, The New York Times, Chicago Tribune, The Washington Post, and the San Jose Mercury News.

CareerPath.com, which initially opened with over 23,000 job listings from these six newspapers, can be searched by individual paper or job category. So what does this comprehensive job listing cost you as an Internet user? It's totally free. That's because the employers are footing the bill.

CareerPath.com is hoping to include other newspapers in its service, as well as a number of other employment services. These will include a bank of electronic resumes, employer and job seeker matching services, company profiles, and alerts that will notify an employer or job seeker when a particular profile of a candidate or opportunity becomes available.

√√ *Personal Web Home Page Ad*

It's not unusual for today's recent college graduates to design and put up on the Internet a Web home page complete with their college graduation picture, interests, and job goals. As described in Chapter 4, you can develop your own Web page, or hire someone to design it for you.

If you're a recent graduate, be sure to include descriptions of courses taken, a personal biography, a resume, and if you've got the grades to back you up, your transcripts.

Even if you're not a recent graduate, a Web page can work for you. Make sure that you include all your accomplishments and experience.

Whatever you do, make your page graphic, interesting, and give the user a reason to contact you. Of course, there are thousands of Web pages and you've got to get the word out. So again, use those listservs and other Internet groups to spread the news.

√√ *Recruitment Pages On-line*

Many Web savvy companies are posting job listings on their Web sites. By using one of the Web's indexing search tools such as Yahoo (**http://www.yahoo.com**), you'll be able to search various corporations and employment sites.

√ *SBA On-line*

The government's Small Business Administration (**http://www.sbaonline.sba.gov**) operates a Web site containing loads of pertinent information about setting up and establishing a business. You'll find guidelines on various programs, as well as numerous helpful hints for taking advantage of programs offered by the SBA.

√ *Usenet Job Listings*

The Usenet is a subset of the Internet. It acts as a bulletin board that organizes thousands of "discussions" which are separated into newsgroups. With Usenet, Internet users can search by pre-defined subjects, regions, and more:

- General business jobs under **misc.jobs.offered**

- Contract positions under **misc.jobs.contract**

- Technical positions under **sci.research.careers**

- Biological sciences under **bionet.jobs**

Government Job Placement

Most states have the equivalent of an Employment Security Office, Labor Department, Department of Human Resources, Jobs Center, Labor Market Information Center, Jobs Bank, or otherwise named organization. The purpose, however, is uniform: To locate jobs and provide skills training. Many of these Employment Security Offices are networked with a national job search called Jobs Bank USA. But first, you must be registered with your local office before gaining access to Jobs Bank USA.

Keep in mind that some of these government departments may also have on-line, searchable databases. So ask for that information if you plan on using a computer.

√√ *Job Placement & Job Training*

Alabama—	334-242-8003	Jobs
Alaska—	907-465-2712	Jobs
Arizona—	602-542-5482	Jobs
Arkansas—	501-682-7675	Jobs
California—	310-782-2100	Jobs
	800-367-2562	Training
Colorado—	303-830-3000	Jobs
Connecticut—	860-566-5160	Jobs
D.C.—	202-939-8739	Jobs
Georgia—	404-656-3017	Jobs
Hawaii—	808-587-0977	Jobs
Idaho—	208-334-6233	Jobs
Illinois—	217-785-5069	Jobs
	312-793-3500	Jobs
Indiana—	317-232-7670	Jobs
Iowa—	515-281-5387	Jobs
Kansas—	913-296-1715	Jobs
	913-271-8787	Training
Kentucky—	502-595-4762	Jobs
Louisiana—	504-342-6600	Jobs
Maine—	207-775-5891	Jobs/Training
Maryland—	410-767-2006	Jobs
Massachusetts—	617-626-6600	Jobs/Training

197

Michigan—	800-285-WORK	Jobs
	517-373-6508	Training
Minnesota—	612-296-2919	Jobs/Training
Mississippi—	610-354-8711	Jobs
	601-949-2003	Training
Missouri—	314-751-4750	Jobs/Training
Montana—	406-228-9369	Jobs
Nebraska—	402-471-2275	Jobs
Nevada—	702-685-8353	Jobs
New Hampshire—	603-224-3311	Jobs
	603-228-9500	Training
New Jersey—	609-292-2323	Jobs
New Mexico—	505-827-7434	Jobs
New York—	518-474-6014	Jobs
North Carolina—	919-733-3941	Jobs
North Dakota—	701-328-5000	Jobs
Ohio—	614-466-2100	Jobs
Oklahoma—	405-557-0200	Jobs
Oregon—	503-225-5555	Ext. 7777 Jobs
Pennsylvania—	717-787-3354	Jobs
Rhode Island—	401-277-3588	Jobs
South Carolina—	803-737-9935	Jobs
South Dakota—	605-626-2314	Jobs
Tennessee—	615-741-2131	Jobs
Texas—	512-475-2149	Jobs
	512-463-2222	Training
Utah—	801-536-7400	Jobs
Vermont—	802-223-7226	Jobs
Virginia—	804-692-0333	Jobs
Washington—	360-407-5100	Jobs
West Virginia—	304-558-2630	Jobs
Wisconsin—	608-266-1731	Jobs
Wyoming—	307-777-3700	Jobs

SOFTWARE & INFORMATION SERVICES

Associations

Business Software Alliance-	Ph: (202) 872-5500
Data Processing Mgt./ Association-	Ph: (708) 825-8124
IEEE Computer Society-	Ph: (202) 371-0101
Information Tech. Assoc. America-	Ph: (703) 522-5055
Software Patent Institute-	Ph: (313) 769-4606
Software Publishers Association-	Ph: (202) 452-1600

Conferences & Tradeshows

Advanstar Exposition- Conferences and shows on voice technology and computer aided design and graphics: 201 East Sandppointe Ave., #600; Santa Ana, CA Ph: (714) 513-8400

The Blenheim Group Expos- Relates to all phases of computer hardware, software and multimedia: One Executive Dr.; Ft. Lee, New Jersey 07024 Ph: (201) 346-1400

CES- Six annual consumer electronic shows including computers and related hardware, software and multimedia from numerous manufacturers, with instructional workshops in many areas: 2500 Wilson Blvd.; Arlington, VA 22201 Ph: (202) 457-8700

Conference Management Corp.- Numerous shows annually specializing in graphics, on-line access and on-line services and products: 200 Connecticut Avenue; Norwalk, CT 06856 Ph: (203) 852-0500

Event Management Services- Ten annual shows covering computer hardware, software and telecommunications: 516 SE Morrison, Suite 500; Portland, OR 97214 Ph: (503) 234-1552

Interface Group- Windows Expo involves software and hardware, networking and numerous related services and tools: 300 First Ave.; Needham, MA 02194 Ph: (617) 449-6953

Interactive Services Association- Two Expos annually dealing with interactive on-line services and telecommunications production: 8403 Colesville Road; Silver Spring, MD 20910 Ph: (301) 495-4955

Knowledge Industry Publications, Inc.- Shows on computer based multimedia and digital video, CD-ROM creation, plus hardware and software manufacturers: 701 Westchester Ave.; White Plains, NY 10604 Ph: (800) 800-5474

Landmark Presentations- Several shows and conferences annually concentrating on computer software and hardware including instructional seminars: 12731 E. Cornell Ave.; Aurora, CO 80014 Ph: (303) 696-6100

MacAcademy- Four annual five day expositions featuring software and hardware for the Macintosh computer, including instruction and computer labs on software, multimedia and 3D graphics: 100 East Granada Blvd.; Ormond Beach, FL 32176-1712 Ph: (800) 527-1914

Maclean Hunter Presentations- Computer software and hardware exhibition: 12731 East Cornell Ave.; Aurora, CO Ph: (303) 751-1880

National Productions, Inc.- Broad spectrum computer Exposition includes exhibits and seminars on software and hardware, the Internet, multimedia and on-line services, computer utilization in education and entertainment: 16175 Monterey Road; Morgan Hill, CA 95037 Ph: (800) 800-5600

NPES- Expo focuses on specialized hardware and software for all types of graphics: 1899 Preston White Dr.; Reston, VA 22091 Ph: (703) 264-7200

Reed Exposition-Expos- Covers a vast array of software, hardware, CD-ROM and multimedia: 383 Main Ave.; Norwalk, CT 06852 Ph: (800) 287-7141

Softbank Comdex- Numerous shows annually concentrating on computer operating systems, software, and Internet: 300 1st Avenue; Needham, MA 02194-2722 Ph: (617) 449-6600

Softbank Exposition- Several shows during the year on software, hardware, and multimedia: 303 Vintage Park Dr.; Foster City, CA 94404 Ph: (800) 488-2883

Usenix- Conferences and tutorials on specialized programming techniques, discussions on system and network security: 22672 Lambert St., Suite 613; Lake Forest, CA 92630 Ph: (714) 588-8649

Ziff Institute- Expo on interactive technologies focusing on related software and hardware: 25 first St.; Cambridge, MA 02141 Ph: (617) 252-5119

Publications

ACM Transactions on Software Engineering and Methodology- Publication focusing on design and development of software: 1515 Broadway, 17th floor: New York, NY 10036-7440 Ph: (212) 869-7440

Authorware- Publication dealing with multimedia software and computer assisted instruction: 600 Townsend St.; San Francisco, CA 94103-4945 Ph: (415) 595-3101

Computer Products News- Ten annual issues presenting new computer hardware and software products from international manufacturers: Pan European Publishing Co.; Rue Verte 216, B-1210 Brussels, Belgium Ph: 32-2-2402611

Computer Users Survival Magazine- Monthly, focused on reviewing and evaluating computer software and hardware: 400 E. 59th St., 9th floor; New York, NY 10022 Ph: (212) 755-4363

Database Programming & Design-Monthly- Magazine that features database development articles: Miller Freeman; 600 Harrison St.; San Francisco, CA 94107 Ph: (415) 905-2200

DBMS- Monthly magazine devoted to hardware and software choices in the business environment: PO Box 469039; Escondido, CA 92046-9039 Ph: (800) 334-8152

Digital News & Review- Bi-weekly publication devoting articles to software, hardware, programming and graphics: 275 Washington St.; Newton, MA 02158-1630 Ph: (617) 964-3030

Dr. Dobb's Journal- Monthly magazine devoted to covering and reviewing the range of software tools for the professional programmer. Miller Freeman, Inc.; 600 Harrison St.; San Francisco, CA 94107 Ph: (415) 905-2200

Graphicommunicator- Eight issues annually featuring articles on both graphic arts and graphic communications: Graphic Communications International Union; 1900 L St. N.W.; Washington, DC 20036 Ph: (202) 462-1400

Graphic Design: USA- Monthly publication dealing with news, opportunities and events in the graphic design field: Kaye Publishing Co.; 1556 Third Ave.; New York, NY 110128 Ph: (212) 534-4415

IEEE Software- Bi-monthly, focusing on programming and software: 10662 Los Vaqueros Circle, Box 3014; Los Alamitos, CA. 90720-1264 Ph: (714) 821-8380

IEEE Transactions on Software Engineering- Publication regarding development and maintenance of computer programs: 345 East 47th St.; New York, NY 10017-2394 Ph: (908) 981-0060

Journal of Systems and Software- Monthly publication which covers all aspects of programming and software design: 655 Avenue of the Americas; New York , NY 10010 Ph: (212) 989-5800

Infoworld- Weekly publication focusing on hardware and software evaluation and new products: 155 Bovet Rd., Suite 800; San Mateo, CA 94402 Ph: (415) 572-7341

Mic/Tech-Mini Computers & Mainframes- Monthly magazine that evaluates and prices computer systems and describes available software: 401 E. Route 70, PO Box 5062; Cherry Hill, NJ 08034 Ph: (609) 428-1020

Packaged Software Reports- Monthly publication focusing on new software products: 401 E. Route 70, Box 5062; Cherry Hill, NJ 08034 Ph: (609) 428-1020

PC Magazine- Publication devoted to information on software for PC's and peripherals: Ziff-Davis Publishing Co.; One Park Ave.; New York, NY 10016 Ph: (212) 503-5100

PC Techniques- Bi-monthly publication concentrating on software and database development: The Coriolis Group; 7721 E. Gray Rd., 204; Scottsdale, AZ 85260 Ph: (602) 483-0192

Software Development Monthly- Monthly publication devoted to software products and techniques: Miller Freeman, Inc.; 600 Harrison St.; San Francisco, CA 94107 Ph: (415) 905-2200

Software Industry Report- Bi-annual publication follows software development worldwide: Computer Age; 3918 Prosperity Ave. #310; Fairfax, VA 22031 Ph: (703) 573-8594

Software Magazine- Monthly magazine dealing with software application and development: Sentry Publishing Company, Inc.; 1900 W. Park Dr.; Westborough, MA 01581 Ph: (508) 366-2031

Software Success- Monthly magazine on software marketing: United Communications Group; 175 Highland Ave; Needham, MA 02194-3034 Ph: (301) 816-8950

Softwatch Quarterly- Quarterly review summarizing articles from over 200 periodicals on software development: Applied Computer Research, Inc.; 11242 N. 19th Ave.; Phoenix, AZ 85029 Ph: (602) 995-5929

Software World- Publication issued bi-monthly and focusing on various types of software programs: A & P Publications, Ltd.; 377 St. John St.; London EC1V4LD, England Ph: 44-71-837-5921

System Development- Monthly newsletter that focuses on improving productivity in system development: Applied Computer Research; PO Box 82266; Phoenix, AZ 85021 Ph: (602) 995-5929

Transactions On Information Systems- Quarterly publication covering communication systems: Association for Computing Machinery; 1515 Broadway, 15th floor; New York, NY 10036-5701 Ph: (212) 869-7440

Training

CES- Six annual consumer electronic shows including computers and related hardware, software and multimedia from numerous manufacturers, together with instructional workshops in many areas: 2500 Wilson Blvd.; Arlington, VA 22201 Ph: (202) 457-8700

City University- Long distance learning for Microsoft Certified Professional certification and other college degrees: City University, Office of Admissions, 919 SW Grady Way; Renton, WA 98055 Ph: (206) 637-1010 & (800) 426-5596 x-3829

Computer Courseware Intl.- Sells courseware manuals for home study of computer applications in a number of operating systems: 20110 Stewart Cr.; Maple Ridge, BC, Canada V2X9E7 Ph: (800) 668-1669

Data-Tech Institute- Annual seminars concentrating on educational training on Macintosh hardware and software: PO Box 2429; Clifton, NJ 07015 Ph: (201) 478-5400

Georgia Tech- One to five day courses dealing with computer programming, multimedia, new computer technology, and the Internet: Department of Continuing Education, Atlanta, GA 30332-0385 Ph: (404) 894-2547

Information Management Network- Intensive 2-day seminars covering database management and direct marketing: 25 West 45th St., Ste. 1505, New York, NY 10036 Ph: (212) 293-7300

Knowledge Systems Corp.- Training in object oriented programming language: 3001 Weston; Cary, NC 27513 Ph: (919) 481-4000

Landmark Presentations- Several shows and conferences annually concentrating on computer software and hardware including instructional seminars: 12731 E. Cornell Ave.; Aurora, CO 80014 Ph: (303) 696-6100

MacAcademy- Four annual five day expositions featuring software and hardware for the Macintosh computer, including instruction and computer labs on software, multimedia and 3D graphics: 100 East Granada Blvd.; Ormond Beach, FL 32176-1712 Ph: (800) 527-1914

National Productions, Inc.- Computer Exposition that includes exhibits and seminars on software and hardware, the Internet, multimedia and on-line services, computer utilization in education and entertainment: 16175 Monterey Road; Morgan Hill, CA 95037 Ph: (800) 800-5600

New Horizon Computer Learning Center- Technical training for the P.C.: 1231 East Dryer Rd.; Santa Ana, CA 92705 Ph: (714) 438-9491

New York University- Courses in telecommunications, multimedia, programming, 3D modeling and animation, World Wide Web, and database marketing: 721 Broadway, 4th Floor; New York, NY 10003-6807 Ph: (212) 998-1880

One Source, Inc.- Training in computer programming, and multimedia use and development: 8-10 West 19th St., 10th floor; New York, NY 10011

Professional Development Institute- Technology certification and employment programs for software, hardware, networking, multimedia, and the Internet: 333 North Wilshire Avenue; Anaheim, CA 92801-5846 Ph: (714) 518-5945 & (800) 333-9002

San Francisco State University- Courses in computer programming, multimedia, telecommunications, and hardware: 1600 Holloway Ave.; San Francisco, CA 94132 Ph: (415) 338-1373

School of Visual Arts- Courses in hardware, software, multimedia, graphic design, animation and virtual reality: Office of Continuing Education, 209 East 23rd Street; New York, NY 10010-3994 Ph: (212) 592-2050

Skillset Training- Training for companies in business computer applications and basic hardware instruction: 69 Younge St.; Toronto, ON, Canada M5E1K3 Ph: (416) 368-1323

Softbank- Conferences for in-house corporate software trainers regarding utilization of business software applications: 10 Presidents Landing; Medford, MA 02115 Ph: (800) 348-7246

Usenix- Conferences and tutorials on specialized programming techniques, discussions on system and network security: 22672 Lambert St., Suite 613; Lake Forest, CA 92630 Ph: (714) 588-8649

HARDWARE

Associations

Computer & Business Equipment Manufacturers Assoc.-
Ph: (202) 737-8888

Computer & Communications Industry Assoc.-
Ph: (202) 783-0070

Computing Technology Industry Association-
Ph: (708) 268-1818

IEEE Computer Society-   Ph: (202) 371-0101

Semiconductor Industry Assoc.-   Ph: (408) 246-2711

Conferences & Tradeshows

CES- Six annual consumer electronic shows including computers and related hardware, software and multimedia from numerous manufacturers, together with instructional workshops in many areas: 2500 Wilson Blvd.; Arlington, VA 22201 Ph: (202) 457-8700

The Blenheim Group- Expos relating to all phases of computer hardware, software and multimedia: One Executive Dr.; Ft. Lee, New Jersey 07024 Ph: (201) 346-1400

Event Management Services- Ten annual shows covering computer hardware, software, and telecommunications: 516 SE Morrison, Suite 500; Portland, Oregon 97214 Ph: (503) 234-1552

Interface Group- Windows Expo involving software and hardware, networking, and numerous related services and tools: 300 First Ave.; Needham, MA 02194 Ph: (617) 449-6953

Knowledge Industry Publications, Inc.- Shows on computer based multimedia and digital video, CD-ROM creation, as well as hardware and software manufacturers: 701 Westchester Ave.; White Plains, NY 10604 Ph: (800) 800-5474

Landmark Presentations- Annual conferences concentrating on software and hardware including instructional seminars: 12731 E. Cornell Ave.; Aurora, CO 80014 Ph: (303) 696-6100

MacAcademy- Four annual five day expositions featuring software and hardware for the Macintosh computer, including instruction and computer labs on software, multimedia, and 3D graphics: 100 East Granada Blvd.; Ormond Beach, FL 32176-1712 Ph: (800) 527-1914

Maclean Hunter Presentations- Computer software and hardware exhibition: 12731 East Cornell Ave.; Aurora, CO Ph: (303) 751-1880

210

Miller Freeman, Inc.- Shows on computer design, microprocessors, and microcontrollers: 600 Harrison St.; San Francisco, CA 94107 Ph: (415) 905-2200

National Productions, Inc.- Broad spectrum computer Expos including exhibits and seminars on software and hardware, the Internet, multimedia and on-line services, computer utilization in education, and entertainment: 16175 Monterey Road; Morgan Hill, CA 95037 Ph: (800) 800-5600

NPES- Expo focusing on specialized hardware and software for all types of graphics: 1899 Preston White Dr.; Reston, VA 22091 Ph: (703) 264-7200

Reed Exposition- Expos covering a vast array of software, hardware, CD-ROM, and multimedia: 383 Main Ave.; Norwalk, CT 06852 Ph: (800) 287-7141

Softbank Comdex- Numerous shows annually concentrating on computer operating systems, software, and Internet: 300 1st Avenue; Needham, MA 02194-2722 Ph: (617) 449-6600

Softbank Exposition- Several shows during the year on software, hardware, and multimedia: 303 Vintage Park Dr.; Foster City, CA 94404 Ph: (800) 488-2883

Ziff Institute- Expo on interactive technologies focusing on related software and hardware: 25 first St.; Cambridge, MA 02141 Ph: (617) 252-5119

Publications

CD-ROM Professional Magazine- Monthly magazine with articles on software and new products: Online Inc., 462 Danbury Rd.; Wilton, CT 06897-2126 Ph: (203) 761-1466

Computercraft- Monthly magazine emphasizing upgrades and repairs on the PC and micro-controllers: CQ Communications, Inc.; 76 N. Broadway; Hicksville, NY 11801 Ph: (516) 681-2922

The Computer Hardware Industry- Annual publication covering full range of hardware from PC to super computer: Dun & Bradstreet Information Services; One Diamond Hill Rd.; Murray Hill, NJ 07974 Ph: (908) 665-5224

Computer Products News- Ten annual issues presenting the newest computer hardware and software products from international manufacturers: Pan European Publishing Co.; Rue Verte 216, B-1210 Brussels, Belgium Ph: 32-2-2402611

Computer Users Survival Magazine- Monthly magazine devoted to reviewing and evaluating computer software and hardware: 400 E. 59th St., 9th floor; New York, NY 10022 Ph: (212) 755-4363

DBMS- Monthly magazine devoted to hardware and software choices in the business environment: PO Box 469039; Escondido, CA 92046-9039 Ph: (800) 334-8152

Digital News & Review- Bi-weekly publication devoting articles to computer software, hardware, programming and graphics: 275 Washington St.; Newton, MA 02158-1630 Ph: (617) 964-3030

Digital Video- Monthly magazine captures latest trends in video, graphics, storage, and teleconferencing, plus includes reviews of new products: Active Media; Inc. 600 Townsend St., San Francisco, CA 94103 (415) 522-2400

Economics Of Multimedia Title Publishing 1995- Details all aspects of the multimedia market from content to financial considerations to marketing: SIMBA Information, Inc.; PO Box 7430, Wilton, CT 06897 Ph: (203) 834-0033 Ext. 178

212

Infoworld- Weekly publication focusing on hardware and software evaluation and new hardware and software products: 155 Bovet Rd., Suite 800; San Mateo, CA 94402 Ph: (415) 572-7341

Mainframe Computing- Monthly magazine concentrating on recent hardware peripherals for mainframe computers, and marketing strategies for mainframe hardware: Worldwide Videotex; Box 3273, Boynton Beach, FL 33424-3273 Ph: (407) 738-2276

Microcomputer Journal- Bi-monthly journal which deals in hardware for the PC and PC upgrading and expanding: CQ Communications, Inc.; 76 N. Broadway; Hicksville, NY 11801 Ph: (516) 681-2922

Mic/Tech-Mini Computers & Mainframes- Monthly magazine evaluates and prices computer systems and available software: 401 E. Route 70, PO Box 5062; Cherry Hill, NJ 08034 Ph: (609) 428-1020

PC Laptop Computers Magazine- Monthly magazine devoted to notebook, hand held and laptop computers: L.F.P. Inc.; 9171 Wilshire Blvd., Suite 300; Beverly Hills, CA 90210 Ph: (310) 858-7155

PC Magazine- Publication devoted to information on software for PC's and peripherals: Ziff-Davis Publishing Co.; One Park Ave.; New York, NY 10016 Ph: (212) 503-5100

Pen Magazine- Bi-monthly publication focusing on pen computing devices: Pen World, Inc.; 761 Deep Valley Rd., Rolling Hills, Estate, CA 90274 Ph: (310) 377-7858

Speech Technology- Quarterly, focusing on voice input-output applications and hardware: Media Dimensions Inc.; 1562 1st St., No. 286; New York, NY 10028-4004 Ph: (212) 533-7481

Training

CES- Six annual consumer electronic shows including computers and related hardware, software and multimedia from numerous manufacturers, with instructional workshops in many areas: 2500 Wilson Blvd.; Arlington, VA 22201 Ph: (202) 457-8700

Data-Tech Institute- Annual seminars concentrating on educational training on Macintosh hardware and software: PO Box 2429; Clifton, NJ 07015 Ph: (201) 478-5400

ITT Technical Institute- Courses and instruction in hardware, communication technology, and virtual reality: 6330 Highway 290 East, Suite 150; Austin, TX 78723 Ph: (512) 467-6800

Landmark Presentations- Several shows and conferences annually concentrating on computer software and hardware including instructional seminars: 12731 E. Cornell Ave.; Aurora, CO 80014 Ph: (303) 696-6100

MacAcademy- Four annual five day expositions featuring software and hardware for the Macintosh computer, including instruction and computer labs on software, multimedia and 3D graphics: 100 East Granada Blvd.; Ormond Beach, FL 32176-1712 Ph: (800) 527-1914

Professional Development Institute- Technology certification and employment programs for software, hardware, networking, multimedia, and the Internet: 333 North Wilshire Avenue; Anaheim, CA 92801-5846 Ph: (714) 518-5945 & (800) 333-9002

San Francisco State University- Offering courses in computer programming, multimedia, telecommunications, and hardware: 1600 Holloway Ave.; San Francisco, CA 94132 Ph: (415) 338-1373

School of Visual Arts- Courses in hardware, software, multimedia, graphic design, animation and virtual reality: Office of Continuing Education, 209 East 23rd Street; New York, NY 10010-3994 Ph: (212) 592-2050

Skillset Training- Training for companies in business computer applications and basic hardware instruction: 69 Younge St.; Toronto, ON, Canada M5E1K3 Ph: (416) 368-1323

Southwest School of Electronics- Courses and instruction in both hardware and communication systems: 5424 Highway 290 West; Austin, TX 78735 Ph: (512) 892-2640

ON-LINE & COMMUNICATIONS SERVICES

Associations

Information Technology Assoc. of America-
Ph: (703) 522-5055

International Communications Assoc.-
Ph: (214) 233-3889

Satellite Broadcasting & Communications Assoc.-
Ph: (703) 549-6990

Society for Technical Communication-
Ph: (703) 522-4114

Telecommunications Industry Association-
Ph: (202) 457-4912

Conferences & Tradeshows

AIC- Conferences on multimedia marketing and distribution and telecommunications: 50 Broad Street, 19th floor; New York, NY 10004 Ph: (800) 409-4242

Argus Trade Shows- Exposition and shows featuring wireless communication: 6151 Powers Ferry Road NW; Atlanta, GA 30339 Ph: (800) 828-0420

CES- Six annual consumer electronic shows including hardware, software, multimedia and communication devices, as well as technology from numerous manufacturers, together with instructional workshops in many areas: 2500 Wilson Blvd; Arlington, VA 22201 Ph: (202) 457-870

Chilton Communications- Expo on interactive television: 600 South Cherry, #400; Denver, CO 80222 Ph: (800) 888-4824

Energy Telecommunications- Telecommunications exhibition featuring a variety of services and products: PO Box 795038; Dallas, TX 75379 Ph: (214) 235-0653

Event Management Services- Ten annual shows covering computer hardware, software and telecommunications: 516 SE Morrison, Suite 500; Portland, OR 97214 Ph: (503) 234-1552

Institute for International Research- One hundred conferences annually covering all phases of telecommunication: 708 3rd Ave.; New York, New York 10017 Ph: (212) 661-8740

Interactive Services Association- Expos covering interactive industry telecommunications production and on-line services: 8403 Colesville Road; Silver Spring, MD 20910 Ph: (301) 495-4955

Jupiter Communications- Shows on cable transmissions, on line devices and hand held notebooks: 594 Broadway; New York, NY 10012 Ph: (212) 780-6060

National Productions, Inc.- Broad spectrum computer Expos including wireless technology, exhibits and seminars on software and hardware, the Internet, multimedia and on-line services, computer utilization in education and entertainment: 16175 Monterey Road; Morgan Hill, CA 95037 Ph: (800) 800-5600

Phillips Business Information- Comprehensive satellite industry conferences: 1201 Seven Locks Road; Potomac, MD 20854 Ph: (800) 777-5006

Softbank Comdex- Numerous shows annually concentrating on computer operating systems, software, and Internet: 300 1st Avenue; Needham, MA 02194-2722 Ph: (617) 449-6600

Publications

Advanced Technology for Developers- Monthly newsletter for data communication designers: High-tech Communications; 103 Buckskin CT; Sewickley, PA 15143-9946 Ph: (412) 741-7699

Communications Technology- Monthly magazine covering cable TV technology: Phillips Business Information, Inc.; 1201 Seven Locks Rd.; Potomac, MD 20854 Ph: (301) 424-3338

Computer Communication- Monthly magazine focusing on communication hardware and software: Turpin Transactions, Ltd. Distribution Centre; Blackhorse Rd, Letchworth, Herts, SG6 1HM England Ph: 0462-672555

Communications Daily- Focusing on all types of electronic communication technologies and emerging techniques: 2115 Ward CT., N.W.; Washington, DC 20037 Ph: (202) 872-9200

Communications Week International- Bi-weekly publication covering the recent news in data communications: CMP Publications; 600 Community Drive; Manhasset, NY 11030 Ph: (516) 365-4600

Communications News- Monthly magazine with articles on all types of video and data transmission technologies and new products on the market: 7500 Old Oak Road; Cleveland, OH 44130 Ph: (216) 243-8100

Data Communications- Monthly publication about new technology for computer networking: McGraw-Hill, Inc.; 1221 Ave. of the Americas; New York, NY 10020 Ph: (212) 512-2000

Digital Video- Monthly magazine captures latest trends in video, graphics, storage, and teleconferencing, plus includes reviews of new products: Active Media; Inc. 600 Townsend St., San Francisco, CA 94103 (415) 522-2400

Employment Opportunities and Job Resources on the Internet- Booklet with tips for using Usenet, Telnet, Gopher sites, Listservs, and the Web: Margaret Riley, Worcester Polytechnic Institute, 100 Institute Rd., Worcester MA 01609 Ph: (508) 831-5410 & http://www.wpi. edu/~mfriley/jobguide.html

Graphicommunicator- Eight issues annually featuring articles on graphic arts and graphic communications: Graphic Communications International Union; 1900 L St. N.W.; Washington, DC 20036 Ph: (202) 462-1400

Internet- Monthly publication reviewing all aspects of internetworking: Horizon House Publications, Inc.; 685 Canton St.; Norwood, MA 02062 Ph: (617) 769-9750

Jupiter Communications- Five newsletters with emphasis on marketing in the Internet: 594 Broadway; New York, NY 10012 Ph: (212) 780-6060

Net- Monthly publication devoted to all aspects of the Internet, with emphasis on facilitating use of the Internet: Imagine Publishing, Inc.; 1350 Old Bayshore Highway, Suite 210; Burlingame, CA 94010 Ph: (415) 696-1661

NetGuide- A monthly, consumer-oriented guide to the Internet and on-line services: CMP Media, Inc; 600 Community Dr., Manhasset, NY 11030 Ph: (516) 562-5000

The Net- Publication focusing entirely on the Internet: Imagine Publishing, Inc.; 1350 Old Bayshore Highway, Suite 210; Burlingame, CA 94010 Ph: (415) 696-1661

Open Systems Communication- Bi-weekly publication dealing with hardware and software integration standards for communication: Phillips Business Information, Inc.; 1201 Seven Lock Rd.; Potomac, MD 20854 Ph: (301) 424-3338

Satellite Week- Weekly Publication focusing on satellite telecommunications: Warren Publishing, Inc.; 2115 Ward CT; Washington, DC 20037 Ph: (202) 872-9200

Space Communications- Quarterly magazine covering all areas of satellite communications: IUS Press; Box 10558; Burke, VA 22009-0558 Ph: (703) 323-5554

Telecommunications- Monthly publication dealing with all aspects of communication: Horizon House Publications, Inc.; 685 Canton St.; Norwood, MA 02062 Ph: (617) 769-9750

Telecommunications and Radio Engineering- Monthly magazine covering all facets of video, digital, optical and analog wire communications: John Wiley & Sons, Inc.; 605 3rd Ave.; New York, NY 110158 Ph: (212) 850-6289

Wireless Data News- Bi-weekly newsletter geared to all forms of wireless transmission: Phillips Business Information, Inc.; 1201 Seven Locks Rd.; Potomac, MD 20854 Ph: (301) 424-3338

Training

CAD Institute- Offers many virtual reality courses including an accredited multimedia and virtual reality degree program: 4100 E. Broadway Rd.; Phoenix, AZ 85024 Ph: (800) 658-5744

Center For Electronic Art- Offers courses and instruction in communication on the Internet, the World Wide Web, and interactive multimedia: 950 Battery Street; San Francisco, CA 94111 Ph: (415) 512-9300

CES- Six annual consumer electronic shows including computers and related hardware, software and multimedia from numerous manufacturers, with instructional workshops in many areas: 2500 Wilson Blvd.; Arlington, VA 22201 Ph: (202) 457-8700

Electronic Visualization Lab- The Electronic Visualization Lab trains students for MS, PhD, and MFA degrees in VR, computer graphics, and interactive techniques: University of Chicago, Chicago, IL 60607-7053: (312) 996-3002 & http://www.ncsa. uiuc.edu/EVL/docs/html/homepage.html

Entertainment Technology Center- The center focuses on training the tomorrow's multimedia experts: University of Southern California, Los Angeles, CA Ph: (213) 740-6207

ITT Technical Institute- Campuses nationwide offering courses and instruction in hardware, communication technology, and virtual reality: 6330 Highway 290 East, Suite 150; Austin, TX 78723 Ph: (512) 467-6800

National Seminars Group- Intensive, one-day Internet workshops at locations around the country: National Seminars Group, 6901 W. 63rd St., P.0. Box 2949, Shawnee Mission, KS 66201-1349 Ph: (800) 258-7246

New York University- Courses in telecommunications, multimedia, programming, 3D modeling and animation, World Wide Web, and database marketing: 721 Broadway, 4th Floor; New York, NY 10003-6807 Ph: (212) 998-1880

Professional Development Institute- Technology certification and employment programs for software, hardware, networking, multimedia, and the Internet: 333 North Wilshire Avenue; Anaheim, CA 92801-5846 Ph: (714) 518-5945 & (800) 333-9002

San Francisco State University- Offering courses in telecommunications, multimedia, computer programming, and hardware: 1600 Holloway Ave.; San Francisco, CA 94132 Ph: (415) 338-1373

School of Visual Arts- Courses in film and video production and camera techniques for network television: 209 East 23rd St.; New York, NY 10010-3994 Ph: (212) 592-2060

Southwest School of Electronics- Courses and instruction in hardware and communication systems: 5424 Highway 290 West; Austin, TX 78735 Ph: (512) 892-2640

CREATIVE SERVICES

Associations

American Society of Journalists and Authors-
Ph: (212) 997-0947

Graphic Communications Association-
Ph: (703) 519-8160

International Interactive Communications Society
Ph: (503) 579-4427

Interactive Multimedia Association- Ph: (410) 626-1380

ITVA- Ph: (214) 869-1112

Conferences & Tradeshows

CES- Six annual consumer electronic shows including computers and related hardware, software and multimedia from numerous manufacturers, with instructional workshops in many areas: 2500 Wilson Blvd.; Arlington, VA 22201 Ph: (202) 457-8700

The Blenheim Group- Expos relating to all phases of computer hardware, software and multimedia: One Executive Dr.; Ft. Lee, New Jersey 07024 Ph: (201) 346-1400

Knowledge Industry Publications, Inc.- Shows covering digital video, CD-ROM, multimedia, hardware, and software: 701 Westchester Ave.; White Plains, NY 10604 Ph: (800) 800-5474

MacAcademy- Four annual expositions featuring software and hardware for Macintosh computers, including instruction and labs on software, multimedia and 3D graphics: 100 East Granada Blvd.; Ormond Beach, FL 32176-1712   Ph: (800) 527-1914

National Productions, Inc.- Exposition that includes exhibits and seminars on software and hardware, the Internet, multimedia, and on-line services, computer utilization in education and entertainment: 16175 Monterey Road; Morgan Hill, CA 95037 Ph: (800) 800-5600

Pseudo On-Line Services- Shows relating to on-line services with an entertainment format: 600 Broadway; New York, NY 20012 Ph: (212) 925-7909

Reed Exposition- Expos covering a vast array of software, hardware, CD-ROM and multimedia: 383 Main Ave.; Norwalk, CT 06852 Ph: (800) 287-7141

Softbank Comdex- Numerous shows annually concentrating on computer operating systems, software, and Internet: 300 1st Avenue; Needham, MA 02194-2722 Ph: (617) 449-6600

Softbank Exposition- Several shows during the year on software, hardware, and multimedia: 303 Vintage Park Dr.; Foster City, CA 94404 Ph: (800) 488-2883

Publications

Authorware- Publication which deals with multimedia software and computer assisted instruction: 600 Townsend St.; San Francisco, CA 94103-4945 Ph: (415) 595-3101

CD-ROM Professional Magazine- Monthly magazine with articles on software and new products: Online Inc., 462 Danbury Rd.; Wilton, CT 06897-2126 Ph: (203) 761-1466

Computer Gaming World- Monthly publication focusing on the most recent developments in computer entertainment: Golden Empire Publications Inc.; 130 S. Chaparral CT, Suite 260; Anaheim CA 92808-2238 Ph: (714) 283-3000

Computer Graphics- Six issues annually devoted entirely to the technology of computer graphics: Technews Ltd, PO Box 626; Kloof 3640 South Africa Ph: 27-31-7640593

Computer Graphics World- Monthly magazine focuses on computer graphics, hardware, and software: Pennwell Publishing Co.; 10 Tara Blvd., 5th floor; Nashua NH 03062-2801 Ph: (603) 891-9156

Digital News & Review- Bi-weekly publication devoting articles to computer software, hardware, programming and graphics: 275 Washington St.; Newton, MA 02158-1630 Ph: (617) 964-3030

Economics Of Multimedia Title Publishing 1995- Details all aspects of the multimedia market from content to financial considerations to marketing: SIMBA Information, Inc.; PO Box 7430, Wilton, CT 06897 Ph: (203) 834-0033 Ext. 178

Electronic Entertainment- Monthly interactive entertainment magazine reviews games, CD-ROM, on-line, and multimedia for PCs and Macs: Infotainment World, Inc.; 951 Mariner's Island Blvd. Ste. 700, San Mateo, CA 94404 Ph: (415) 349-4300

Electronic Musician- Monthly magazine covering latest in MIDI, computer-related musical equipment and software: Cardinal Business Media, Inc.; 6400 Hollis St. #12, Emeryville, CA 94608 Ph: (510) 653-3307

Game Informer Magazine- Bi-monthly magazine reviewing video game hardware and software: Sunrise Publications; 10120 W. 76th St.; Eden Prairie, MN 55344 Ph: (612) 946-7245

Graphicommunicator- Eight issues annually featuring articles on graphic arts and graphic communications: Graphic Communications International Union; 1900 L St. N.W.; Washington, DC 20036 Ph: (202) 462-1400

Graphic Design: USA- Monthly publication includes news, opportunities and events in the field: Kaye Publishing Co.; 1556 Third Ave.; New York, NY 110128 Ph: (212) 534-4415

InterActivity- Bi-monthly magazine focuses on all the how-to aspects of designing and developing interactive multimedia, including books, games, and TV products: Miller Freeman, Inc.; 600 Harrison St., San Francisco, CA 94107 Ph: (415) 905-2200

Journal of Imaging Science And Technology- Bi-monthly publication devoted to research and development in imaging: IS&T: Society for Imaging Science & Technology; 7003 Kilworth La.; Springfield, VA 22151 Ph: (703) 642-9090

Multimedia Business Report- Weekly multimedia industry news from new products to marketing strategies: SIMBA Information, Inc.; PO Box 7430, Wilton, CT 06897 Ph: (203) 834-0033 Ext. 178

MultiMedia Schools-Digital Video- Monthly magazine captures latest trends in video, graphics, storage, and teleconferencing, plus includes reviews of new products: Active Media; Inc. 600 Townsend St., San Francisco, CA 94103 (415) 522-2400

MultiMedia Schools- Published five times yearly, the magazine serves as a practical journal of CD-ROM, multimedia, on-line, and Internet for K-12: Online, Inc.; 462 Danbury Road, Wilton, CT 06897-2126 Ph: (203) 761-1466

Multimedia Source Book- Directory listing over 6,000 manufacturers, services, products, and talent in the multimedia industry: Hi-Tech Media, Inc.; 445 Fifth Avenue, New York, NY 10016 Ph: (212) 293-3900

Net- Monthly publication devoted to the Internet, with emphasis on facilitating use of the Internet: Imagine Publishing, Inc.; 1350 Old Bayshore Highway, Suite 210; Burlingame, CA 94010 Ph: (415) 696-1661

The Net- Publication focusing entirely on the Internet: Imagine Publishing, Inc.; 1350 Old Bayshore Highway, Suite 210; Burlingame, CA 94010 Ph: (415) 696-1661

New Media- Monthly magazine includes in-depth reviews of authoring programs, hardware, software, and entertainment: Hypermedia Communications, Inc.; 901 Mariner's Island Blvd., Suite 365, San Mateo , CA 94404 Ph: (415) 573-5170

Videography- Monthly magazine giving an analysis of the video industry: PSN Publications; 2 Park Ave, 8th Floor; New York, NY 10016 Ph: (212) 213-3444

Training

American Film Institute- Seminars and classes on multimedia, film, video, digital media, and marketing a multimedia product: 2021 N. Western Ave.; Los Angeles, CA 90027 Ph: (213) 856-7690

CAD Institute- Offers many multimedia and graphics courses including the first degree program for any college in multimedia and virtual reality: 4100 E. Broadway Rd.; Phoenix, AZ 85024 Ph: (800) 658-5744

Center For Electronic Art- Classes in animation, multimedia, art related computer applications and desktop publishing: 950 Battery Street; San Francisco, CA 94111 Ph: (415) 512-9300

CES- Six annual consumer electronic shows including computers and related hardware, software and multimedia from numerous manufacturers, with instructional workshops in many areas: 2500 Wilson Blvd.; Arlington, VA 22201 Ph: (202) 457-8700

Design Systems- Computer training on multimedia and 3D animation: 37 E. 7 St.; New York, NY Ph: (212) 995-8494

Georgia Tech- One to five day courses dealing with computer programming, multimedia, new computer technology, and the Internet: Department of Continuing Education, Atlanta, GA 30332-0385 Ph: (404) 894-254

International Film & TV Workshops- Training in areas of digital computer, film and video: 2 Central St.; Rockport, ME 04856 Ph: (207) 236-8581

ITP- Courses in multimedia and related topics: 721 Broadway; New York, NY 10003 Ph: (212) 998-1880

MacAcademy- Four annual five day expositions featuring software and hardware for the Macintosh computer, including instruction and computer labs on software, multimedia and 3D graphics: 100 East Granada Blvd.; Ormond Beach, FL 32176-1712 Ph: (800) 527-191

New York University- Offering courses in telecommunications, multimedia, programming, 3D modeling and animation, World Wide Web, and database marketing: 721 Broadway, 4th Floor; New York, NY 10003-6807 Ph: (212) 998-1880

One Source, Inc.- Training in computer programming, and multimedia use and development: 8-10 West 19th St., 10th floor; New York, NY 10011

Parsons School of Design- Classes in computer illustration and design applications in certain select industries: 2 West 13th St.; New York, NY 10011 Ph: (212) 229-8900

Platt College- Instruction in computer drafting, computer graphics and design: 6250 El Cajon Blvd.; San Diego, CA 92115 Ph: (619) 265-0107

Professional Development Institute- Technology certification and employment programs for software, hardware, networking, multimedia, and the Internet: 333 North Wilshire Avenue; Anaheim, CA 92801-5846 Ph: (714) 518-5945 & (800) 333-9002

San Francisco State University- Courses in computer programming, multimedia, telecommunications and hardware: 1600 Holloway Ave.; San Francisco, CA 94132 Ph: (415) 338-1373

School of Communication Arts- Courses in computer art, animation, graphics, multimedia, and video production technology: 2526 27th Ave. South; Minneapolis, MN 55406 Ph: (612) 721-5357

School of Visual Arts- Courses in hardware, software, multimedia, graphic design, animation, and virtual reality: Office of Continuing Education, 209 East 23rd Street; New York, NY 10010-3994 Ph: (212) 592-2050

ADVERTISING & MARKETING

Associations

American Marketing Association-   Ph: (312) 648-0536

Assoc. for Innovative Marketing-   Ph: (617) 784-1747

Data Interchange Standards Assoc.- Ph: (703) 548-7005

Direct Marketing Association-   Ph: (212) 768-7277

Marketing Research Association-   Ph: (203) 257-4008

Conferences & Tradeshows

AIC- Shows on marketing, and distribution of multimedia: 50 Broad Street, 19th fl; New York, NY 10004 Ph: (800) 409-4242

Cowles Business Media- Data base marketing and copywriting conferences: Box 4232; Stamford, CT 06907 Ph: (203) 358-9900

CMC- Numerous shows annually specializing in on-line access and on-line services and products: 200 Connecticut Avenue; Norwalk , CT 06856 Ph: (203) 852-0500

CreaTech- Interactive advertising, marketing and promotion: 91 Highland Road; Scarsdale, NY 10012 Ph: (914) 723-4464

Global Business Research- Expos on Internet advertising: 151 West 19th St., 8th floor; New York, NY 10011 Ph: (800) 868-7188

National Seminars Group- Numerous Internet seminars, with workshops in marketing: 6901 W. 63rd St., PO Box 2949; Shawnee Mission, KS 66201-1349 Ph: (800) 258-7246

Skillpath- Annual shows on the Internet, including advertising, marketing, and customer services: 6900 Squibb Rd., Suite 300; Mission KS 66201 Ph: (800) 873-7545

Publications

Advertising- Monthly publication featuring advertising and marketing programs: Advertising/Communications Times, Inc.; 121 Chestnut St.; Philadelphia, PA 19106 Ph: (215) 629-1666

Advertising Age- Weekly newspaper dealing with worldwide news in the area of marketing and advertising: 740 N. Rush St.; Chicago, IL 60611 Ph: (312) 649-5200

Computer Marketing Newsletter- Monthly publication on the computer sales industry: MV Publishing Inc.; Box 3649; Newport Beach, CA 92659-8649 Ph: (714) 548-9151

The CyberMarketing Letter- Monthly Publication devoted entirely to on-line marketing: 284 Palisades Ave.; Dobbs Ferry, NY 10522 Ph: (914) 693-5950

Directory of Computer & Software Retailers- Lists over 400 computer and software distributors: CSG Information Services; 3922 Coconut Palm Dr.; Tampa, FL 33619 Ph: (813) 664-6800

Economics of Multimedia Title Publishing 1995- Details the entire multimedia market from content to marketing: SIMBA Information, Inc.; PO Box 7430, Wilton, CT 06897 Ph: (203) 834-0033 Ext. 178

Jupiter Communications- Five newsletters with emphasis on marketing in the Internet: 594 Broadway; New York, NY 10012 Ph: (212) 780-6060

Journal Of Marketing- Quarterly publication dealing with marketing practices and new marketing techniques: 250 S. Wacker Dr.; Chicago, IL 60606 Ph: (312) 648-0536

Mainframe Computing- Monthly magazine concentrating on recent hardware peripherals and marketing strategies for mainframe computers: Worldwide Videotex; Box 3273, Boynton Beach, FL 33424-3273 Ph: (407) 738-2276

Multimedia Business Report- Weekly industry news from new products to marketing strategies: SIMBA Information, Inc.; PO Box 7430, Wilton, CT 06897 Ph: (203) 834-0033 Ext. 178

Software Success- Monthly magazine on software marketing: United Communications Group; 175 Highland Ave; Needham, MA 02194-3034 Ph: (301) 816-8950

Telecommunication- Monthly marketing newsletter for all mobile and satellite communications: PO Box 2643; George Downes Dr.; Bucketty N.S.W. 2250 Australia Ph: 61-49-988744

Training

American Film Institute- Offering classes on multimedia, film, video, digital media, and marketing a multimedia product: 2021 N. Western Ave.; Los Angeles, CA 90027 Ph: (213) 856-7690

Cowles Business Media- Database marketing and copywriting conferences, including tutorials and educational forums on database marketing, design and strategy: Box 4232; Stamford, CT 06907 Ph: (203) 358-9900

Electronic University Network- Long distance learning network with MBA and BS in Computer Systems, programming, networking, and marketing. Open Learning Systems, Inc.; 1977 Coestin Road, Hornbrook, CA 96044 Ph: (800) 225-3276

Information Management Network- Intensive 2-day seminars covering database management and direct marketing: 25 West 45th St., Ste. 1505, New York, NY 10036 Ph: (212) 293-7300

National Seminars Group- Seminars on the Internet, with workshops in marketing products and services: 6901 W. 63rd St., PO Box 2949; Shawnee Mission, KS 66201 Ph: (800) 258-7246

New York University- Courses in multimedia, programming, telecommunications, 3D modeling, animation, World Wide Web, and database marketing: 721 Broadway, 4th Fl.; New York, NY 10003 Ph: (212) 998-1880

Skillpath- Several shows annually focusing on the Internet, including advertising and marketing and customer services: 6900 Squibb Rd., Suite 300; Mission KS 66201 Ph: (800) 873-7545

VIRTUAL REALITY

Associations

Computer & Business Equipment Manufacturers Assoc.-
Ph: (202) 737-8888

Digital Multimedia Association-   Ph: (619) 685-2068

IEEE Computer Society-   Ph: (202) 371-0101

International Interactive Communications Society
Ph: (503) 579-4427

Interactive Multimedia Association- Ph: (410) 626-1380

Software Publishers Association-   Ph: (202) 452-1600

Conferences & Tradeshows

Amusitronix- Annual virtual reality exhibition (sometimes limited to commercial users) and equipment rental availability: 141-15 70th Rd.; Flushing, NY 11367 Ph: (718) 268-4411

Interactive Conference- SkillTech Professional Seminars Ph: (800) 348-7246

Multimedia Expo- Expo covering all aspects of multimedia production and services, including lectures and seminars: American Expositions, 110 Greene Street, New York, NY 10012 Ph: (212) 226-4141

VR Expo- Comprehensive virtual reality conference and exhibition including lectures, workshops and tutorials on virtual reality hardware and software: Mecklermedia; 20 Ketchum Street; Westport, CT 06880 Ph: (800) 632-5537

Publications

Cypher Edge Journal- Bi-monthly publication having a broad based coverage of virtual reality: No. 1 Gate Six Road, Suite 6; Sausalito, CA 94965 Ph: (415) 331-3343

Electronic Entertainment- Monthly, interactive entertainment magazine previews and reviews games, CD-ROM, on-line, and multimedia for PCs and Macs: Infotainment World, Inc.; 951 Mariner's Island Blvd. Ste. 700, San Mateo, CA 94404 Ph: (415) 349-4300

Multimedia Source Book- Directory listing over 6,000 manufacturers, services, products, and talent in the multimedia industry: Hi-Tech Media, Inc.; 445 Fifth Avenue, New York, NY 10016 Ph: (212) 293-3900

New Media- Monthly magazine includes in-depth reviews of multimedia authoring programs, hardware, software, and entertainment: Hypermedia Communications, Inc.; 901 Mariner's Island Blvd., Suite 365, San Mateo, CA 94404 Ph: (415) 573-5170

Pix-Elation- Publication to become an on-line product only dealing with all phases of virtual reality: VRASP; PO BOX 4139, Highland Park, NJ 08904 Ph: (908) 463-8787

Virtual Reality Marketplace- Annual publication listing products, services, and companies found in the virtual reality industry: Mecklermedia, 20 Ketchum Street; Westport, CT 06880 Ph: (203) 226-6967

Virtual Reality Special Report- Monthly publication dealing with virtual reality development and cyber space: Miller Freeman, Inc.; 600 Harrison St.; San Francisco, CA 94107 Ph: (415) 905-2200

VR News- Publication focusing on virtual reality : Cydata Ltd.; PO Box 2515; London 4 4JW UK Ph: 44-81L-921498

VR World- Bi-monthly magazine designed for developers and users of virtual reality, it includes reviews of new VR products, software, and hardware: Mecklermedia Corporation; 20 Ketchum Street, Westport, CT 06880 Ph: (203) 226-6967

Training

American Film Institute- Offering classes on multimedia, film, video, digital media, and marketing a multimedia product: 2021 N. Western Ave.; Los Angeles, CA 90027 Ph: (213) 856-7690

CAD Institute- Offers many virtual reality courses including an accredited multimedia and virtual reality degree program: 4100 E. Broadway Rd.; Phoenix, AZ 85024 Ph: (800) 658-5744

Electronic Visualization Lab- The Electronic Visualization Lab trains students for MS, PhD, and MFA degrees in VR, computer graphics, and interactive techniques: University of Chicago, Chicago, IL 60607-7053: (312) 996-3002 & http://www.nc sa.uiuc.edu/EVL/docs/html/homepage.html

Entertainment Technology Center- The center focuses on training the tomorrow's multimedia experts: University of Southern California, Los Angeles, CA Ph: (213) 740-6207

ITT Technical Institute- Courses in hardware, communication technology, and virtual reality (Indiana location): 6330 Highway 290 East, Suite 150; Austin, TX 78723 Ph: (512) 467-6800

Mecklermedia Conference Management- Comprehensive virtual reality conference and exhibition including lectures and workshops on virtual reality hardware and software: 20 Ketchum Street; Westport, CT 06880 Ph: (800) 632-5537

School of Communication Arts- Courses in computer art, animation, graphics, multimedia, and video technology: 2526 27th Ave. South; Minneapolis, MN 55406 Ph: (612) 721-5357

School of Visual Arts- Courses in hardware, software, multimedia, graphic design, animation and virtual reality: Office of Continuing Education, 209 East 23rd Street; New York, NY 10010-3994 Ph: (212) 592-2050

University of Central Florida- Offers an undergraduate and a graduate program in virtual reality: Computer Science Department; Computer Center 2, Room 205; Orlando, FL 32816-2362 Ph: (407) 823-2341

University Applied Physics Laboratory- Virtual reality research and a program in interdivisional sensory engineering for medical, training, and military applications: John Hopkins University, Baltimore, MD Ph: (301) 953-6211

INDEX

C (Cont.)

computer security 62
   security specialist 34
consumer on-line services 144
   number of subscribers 94
copy writer 145
copyright 42
creative services 25, 119, 223
customer service 144
cyber cop 63
cyber researcher 110
cyber journalist 111

D

data communications analyst 35, 95
database consultant 35, 48
database management templates 55
desktop publishing 36
desktop video 46
Dialog 110
digital certification 64
digital film studio 129
digital imaging 176
digital phone lines 12
digital video 82
direct marketing 155
Dow Jones News/Retrieval 110

E

E-mail 144
E-mail lists 160
educator 95
edutainment 120
electronic books 40
electronic data interchange 144, 147
electronic publishing 40
electronic rights specialist 126
employment security office 195
encryption technology 64

entrepreneur 35, 95, 164

F

FedWorld 192
fiber-optic cable 89
film/video producer 121
filmmaker 42

G

game designer 121, 137
game developer 164
game server franchise 140
game tester 137
games 166
   revenues 136
graphic designer 35, 95, 103, 121, 130, 148, 168
groupware 50-51

H

hard disk storage 84
hardware 23, 65, 207
   market share 23
hybrid CD-ROM 70
hypertextbooks 107

I

ID Chips 81
industrial designer 95
information management 48
information services 21, 197
   market share 21
instructional designer 96, 121
interactive ad agency 149
interactive advertising 148
interactive card decks 155
interactive catalogs 61
interactive comics 132
interactive designer 130
interactive designer 121
interactive marketing 26
Interactive Mktg Institute 148
interactive movie 138

242

V

video editor 46
video game technician 165, 166
video producer 35
video-on-demand 96
videoconferencing 7, 112
    revenues 112
videoconferencing director 116
videographer 42-43
virtual actor 167
virtual architect 170
virtual art exhibits 166
virtual art galleries 8
virtual medicine 176
virtual objects 171
virtual office parks 174
virtual photo store 172
virtual photographer 182
virtual photography 181
virtual psychotherapy 177
virtual reality 27, 163, 236
    entertainment centers 167
virtual sales presentations 173
virtual set design 168
virtual set designer 169
virtual training 175
VRML (Virtual Reality
Modeling Language) 180

W

World Wide Web 9, 29, 101
    web farmer 101-102
    web link artist 159
    web marketing software
    152
    web page designer 103,
    145
    web publisher 165
    web site 45
        designer 45
    web software 104
        revenues 104
wide area networks 48
wired communications 90

wireless communications 90
women-owned companies 18
workforce trends 13
writer 35, 122
writing templates 38